Revolution and Regeneration

Revolution and Regeneration

*Life Cycle and the Historical
Vision of the Generation of 1776*

PETER CHARLES HOFFER

The University of Georgia Press
Athens

Designed by Francisca Vassy
Set in 10 on 13 point Palatino
Printed in the United States of America

The paper in this book meets the guidelines for
permanence and durability of the Committee
on Production Guidelines for Book Longevity of
the Council on Library Resources.

Library of Congress Cataloging in Publication Data

Hoffer, Peter C.
Revolution and regeneration.
Includes bibliographical references.
1. United States—Intellectual life—1783–1865.
2. Revolutionists—United States—Psychology. 3. States-
men—United States—Psychology. 4. Life cycle, Human.
5. Psychohistory. 6. United States—Historiography.
I. Title.
E164.H7 1983   973.3   82-24728
ISBN 0-8203-0667-3

For Natalie

*whose time has come
to shine*

We live in a day, when one year of life is worth many in dull common times . . . to say nothing about the convention of an empire to give features to a nation . . . we have a world of curiosity in our own commonwealth. Some characters render themselves the wonder of all who have the powers of wondering at anything in these times.

JAMES SULLIVAN TO RUFUS KING, 1787

The idea is to deal with history, not as a list of historians to be estimated in terms of some standard of excellence, but to deal with the ideas of history, at any time as part of, and influenced by, the general preconceptions and ideas of that time.

CARL LOTUS BECKER, 1933

Contents

Preface

Fifty years after Charles Beard's address to the American Historical Association, it is surely a cliché to say that every generation writes its own history. Each generation has its own visions and needs, which its version of history expresses. The theme of *Revolution and Regeneration* is that a single generation writes its own history many times, as its spokesmen grow older. As the "generation of 1776" matured, they faced a series of crises and opportunities. Their ideas of history—particularly their own earliest exploits—changed as they confronted these episodes in their lives. Their intellectual struggle to fit their understanding of America's past to changing personal circumstances was a vital exercise for them and is a neglected subject today. The shifting notions of history in their private researches and public expressions beckons the historian of ideas and the psychohistorian. *Revolution and Regeneration* attempts a marriage of these two approaches.

To explain how the young revolutionaries of 1776 arrived at the particular intellectual solutions they embraced and to identify the uniformities in those solutions, I have borrowed a concept well known in social and developmental psychology: life cycle. The notion of "stages" of adult maturation employed in this book has the same heuristic value as concepts of role behavior and status consciousness in social history, economies of scale in economic history, and reference groups in political history. Psychohistory is the use of a set of tools—psychological concepts, findings, and insights—to explain human behavior and thought; in this case, the turnings and twistings of the younger revolutionaries' views of American history. The approach succeeds—the methods prove their worth—if the reader feels a little more enlightened about the deepest meanings of the historical ideas of this generation.

I gratefully acknowledge the assistance of the staffs of the Widener, Houghton, and Lamont Libraries of Harvard University, the Boston Public Library, the Library of Congress, the Butler Library of Columbia University, and the University Libraries of Notre Dame and Georgia. This book has had a long gestation, during which I have turned to teachers, colleagues, and friends for guidance. Chief among these are the hardy souls who undertook to read and emend various versions of the manuscript. My thanks go to Bernard Bailyn, Mary Young, John C. Burnham, Alden Vaughan, Michael Kammen, Peter Shaw, and N. E. H. Hull for their perceptive comments and gentle criticisms through the years. To Paul Nagel and Lester Stephens, successive heads of the University of Georgia Department of History, and William Owens and Abraham Tesser of the university's Institute for Behavioral Research, all of whom arranged for released time for me to complete this project, my gratitude is equally great. A grant from the Office of the Vice-President for Research of the University of Georgia made possible the inclusion of the portraits of Adams, Jefferson, Madison, and Hamilton, and I would like to thank Vice-President Robert C. Anderson for this assistance. Michael Justus performed wonders checking citations and quotations in the text. Karen Orchard coordinated the editing with skill, patience, and dispatch. Charles East, editor of the University of Georgia Press, kept faith with this project when its author's spirit flagged. Such a debt is easily acknowledged but impossible to repay.

Revolution and Regeneration

Life Cycle and the Revolutionary Generation

Revolution and Regeneration is a book about the tie between ideas and human experience. Human intellectual activity is inseparable from human experience. Ideas are our groping for mastery over our world, our means of sharing feelings and knowledge with each other and transmitting them to new generations. Ideas may survive the ravages of time that carry off their creators, but the thought must always be interpreted within the context of the thinker. No matter how correct the ideas may seem to us or how universal they aspire to be, their historical explanation lies within the orbit of those who set them down.

What do we know about our own lives that throws light upon the connection between ideas and human experience? Although our minds are genetically predisposed to receive information even before our birth, our store of knowledge comes from our experience. As we grow older, our ability to make sense of the "blooming, buzzing" confusion of the outside world increases. Yet even as our exposure to the world expands, our ideas about the world, the frameworks into which we fit new bits of experience, stiffen. With advancing age, we resist wholesale alteration or correction of our ideas. Intellectual history may be characterized as a sorting out of these two processes of change and persistence.

Although historians have proffered many explanations of change and persistence in our intellectual past, a central fact in our experience is often overlooked. Our ideas are influenced by our stage in life. Historians have begun to explore aging in Western civilization; it is only a matter of time until the relationship between aging and intellectual life is systematically added to this body of literature. But where to begin? This book is an exploratory essay—a first look into that linkage. In it, I explore a basic association between the ideas of a generation of Americans and their maturation, from youth to old age. The model for aging is taken from the work of Erik Erikson and David Levinson, the subjects are the younger revolutionaries of 1776, and the set of ideas examined are the revolutionaries' notions of history—including their place in it.

Any method of insight a historian borrows from another discipline should be theoretically congenial to the way historians work. The new hypothesis or result must purport to explain observable human behavior. Many psychological instruments and methodologies touch upon aging and cognition, but none is more consonant with the historian's own methods than the notion of life cycle. Erik Erikson's recreation of the inner life of his subjects complements the style of professional historians, and his formal program of life-cycle events has been used to measure the progress of individuals in past time. His four categories of adult ego development focus upon distinct "challenges." A youth faces the challenge of finding an identity for himself, distinct from his role as a child yet integrated with his past experience. The young adult must choose between intimacy and the sacrifice of self to others it entails, or isolation, with its potential for self-destruction. The mature individual can maintain his creativity, passing a lifetime of experience on to a new generation, or stagnate. The old man faces the task of achieving a sense of pride in self, an "ego integrity"—or falling into the snare of "feeling that this one chance has been wasted and has, in essence, been worthless."[1]

The connection between life-cycle studies and historical research should be underlined: it is the stuff of which history is made. Life cycle is the passage of individuals through recognizable periods of adjustment and growth, both internally and (here is where it differs from Freudian depth psychology) externally. Early adulthood, the last portion of the struggle of the child to determine who he is, brings with it the end of formal education, living with parents, uncertainty about career, and opens the opportunity to join in adult group activities. Full adulthood finds the individual establishing his career and family, "making it" in the outside world. This is the notion of "intimacy" Erikson introduced in *Childhood and Society* (1953). He stressed the emotional affinities that blossom in this stage of age, certainly an important part of maturation. Later adulthood places the older individual at the head of a family and at the same time enjoins upon him the responsibilities of passing on customs, values, and property to a new generation. Erikson called this "generativity"; David Levinson prefers the term "mentoring"; in modern child guidance manuals one finds the word "parenting." The meaning is the same. Old age brings with it the imminence of death. In early America, as in all traditional societies, great age conferred status. Those who had learned the secret of survival were highly esteemed. Modern Western nations do not do homage to their elderly, perhaps because there are so many more of them. Whatever worth a culture assigns to its oldest members, the old find themselves faced with the ultimate question: were their lives well spent? The old act out these self-judgments. They tell stories of how it once was; they give advice to others; they write preambles to wills and pronounce valedictories before comrades and co-workers. All of this, from young adulthood to very old age, is the proper subject of historical study. Life cycle is not a model we fabricate and then impose upon the past. It is a reality we now discern.[2]

Where then to begin to explore the connection between life's cycles and human ideas? For the American historian in this era of bicentennials one choice stands out, and, indeed, scholars have always regarded the founding of the republic as a pivotal event in our nation's history. To the revolutionaries themselves, it seemed little short of miraculous that a great nation could emerge from scattered outposts of the British Empire on the shores of a vast wilderness. And what a nation it seemed to be: the asylum of Europe's liberty, enterprise, and virtue; the home of a new species of man and woman. Out of these events—of revolution, constitutionmaking, and the establishment of a democratic republican system—emerged ideas that have stood for "America" for more than two hundred years.

For almost the entire span of time between the crisis of the 1760s and the period following the War of 1812, the same cast of characters directed public affairs and intellectual activities. They left parents and home to find a life in the Revolution, matured into lawmakers, party leaders, and men of letters, and departed as old and honored Founding Fathers. The Adamses and Jeffersons, Rushes and Kings, Jays and Pickerings, Freneaus and Websters were a generation that was born and matured with the republic. To be sure, only a few of them held office or published before the collapse of British rule; they were the movement's young recruits and its beneficiaries.[3] Even within their number, the youngest revolutionaries of 1776 do not constitute a birth cohort. Alexander Hamilton, barely eighteen, joined with such older leaders as John Adams and Thomas Jefferson to ensure the success of the venture. When one calls this collection of men a generation, one means that they shared essentially the same formative historical experiences, that their lives were decisively shaped by the same historical events.[4] They are, in this study,

4

a selected composite. In comparable fashion, Stanley Elkins and Eric McKitrick portrayed the federalists of 1787 as the "young men of the revolution," and David Hackett Fischer distinguished between "young Federalists" and "old Federalists"—not meaning to describe the precise mean age of their subjects so much as to delineate a set of shared expectations and needs.[5] The historical generation of 1776 possessed a certain outlook, a view of the world, "a collective identity," which earlier or later generations, whose lives and opinions had been shaped by other historical events, did not share. As Pauline Maier has written, they served an "apprenticeship" in the crisis.[6]

This "historical generation" of 1776 is defined by subjective personal experience. In it one may include those men young enough in 1776 to have been deeply influenced by the crisis and old enough to have taken some part in it, but not those patriots already established in their ways and identities before the crisis swept over them. Such voluble leaders as Richard Henry Lee and Roger Sherman were too old and too settled in 1776 for the uprising to be a formative period in their coming of age. On the other end of the age scale, John Quincy Adams and Andrew Jackson, though they lived through the horrors of the war, were too young to take mature parts in the upheaval and thus too young to include in this group. Their formative years coincided with the party quarrels of the 1790s. John Adams, born in 1735, presents, as usual, a problem. Forty-one in the year of independence, he was married and had established his legal practice in his native colony. Yet he admitted in his diaries and his autobiography that he became an adult in the midst of the imperial controversies of the early 1760s, in fact, as a direct result of those events. His youthful search for identity thus overlapped with and became inseparable from the political crisis. Adams proves to be a singular case. Pennsylvania revolutionary leader Thomas McKean, born a year earlier than Adams, came to maturity in the 1750s, too early to fit the generation of 1776. Elias Boudinot of New Jersey, born in 1740, five years after Adams, was "a person of consequence" in the colony by 1772, when he took young Alexander Hamilton under his wing. Unlike Hamilton, he had reached maturity before the onset of the final crisis. The case of Jeremy Belknap is slightly different but typical of another group of men excluded "for cause." Belknap was born in 1744, of a middle-class Boston family, and educated at Harvard. From his first written work to his death in 1798, he loved revolutionary history and promoted scholarly projects. He was also a patriot, occasionally serving as chaplain for revolutionary troops and preaching pro-independence sermons. Yet his formative years were spent far from the scenes of crisis, in service to a Dover, New Hampshire, congregation. He matured by overcoming other challenges than those posed by English repression and found his identity in his religious calling and scholarly avocation. Though a member of the birth cohort of the generation of 1776, he was not one of them.[7]

Our young revolutionaries matured in the years of crisis, in the midst of crisis. The Revolution was their coming of age. So defined, the older members of the generation of 1776 traced in this book include Hugh Henry Brackenridge (b. 1748), Elbridge Gerry (b. 1744), John Jay (b. 1745), Thomas Jefferson (b. 1743), Timothy Pickering (b. 1745), Benjamin Rush (b. 1745), and James Wilson (b. 1742). Among the younger of the "young men of the Revolution" followed most closely are Fisher Ames (b. 1758), Joel Barlow (b. 1754), Timothy Dwight (b. 1752), Philip Freneau (b. 1752), Alexander Hamilton (b. 1757), David Humphreys (b. 1752), Rufus King (b. 1755), James Madison (b. 1751), John Marshall (b. 1755), Gouverneur Morris (b. 1752), David Ramsay (b. 1749), Edmund Randolph (b. 1753), and Noah Webster (b. 1758). All, with the exception of Adams, were born between 1742 and 1758.

My enumeration of the young men of 1776 is hardly exhaustive. According to Robert Wells, there were about 2.2 million persons in the thirteen colonies on the eve of the rebellion. The mean sex ratio was in the vicinity of 1.20—that is, twelve men for every ten women. Of the total population, about 45.5 percent were children. Therefore, about 665,000 adult males were available as recruits to the revolutionary cause. Let us conservatively estimate that one-fifth of these men did elect to become active revolutionaries: a mass of 133,000. If the overall colonial age distribution held in the revolutionary camp, about 25 percent of these men would have been over thirty-four years in age. This is a most speculative estimate, but it does not matter very much if it is wrong by as many as five percentage points either way. Once the older revolutionaries have been subtracted, we are still left with 100,000 young men. All of these men had hopes and fears, views of their world which they shared with their comrades, but only a few became noted for their ideas, even among their friends, and fewer still left any record of their thoughts. Intellectual history is often a sampling of the ideas of very few. The young men of the Revolution named above and followed below are drawn from an elite—selected by their own talents, by the recognition of their peers, and by the contingencies of long life. Lest I be accused of embracing a "trickledown" philosophy of history, I hurry to remind the reader that the men in this study came from both poles of the late eighteenth-century ideological spectrum. Though their life course was similar, they were not uniform in their politics or their loyalties (save to the republic). Some knew each other well—Madison, Brackenridge, and Freneau at Princeton; Barlow, Webster, Humphreys, and Dwight at Yale; Hamilton, Randolph, and Madison at the Constitutional Convention—and almost all of them crossed the paths of the others at various times in their careers. They were not a band or bloc, for all their common experience and ambition, but a cross-section of the intellectual elite of a generation whose leaders worked in close touch with each other.[8]

Most important for our purposes, these were all men who took the time and made the effort to try to sort out their place in the revolutionary society they made. They were self-conscious intellectuals, as well as legislators, judges, poets, editors, doctors, lawyers, and men of affairs. With justice one may call these men the revolutionary generation; they were among its leaders and interpreters to the world. More important, it was a formative event for them. Such a responsibility invariably becomes reciprocal, and the revolutionaries wove pieces of their private lives into the larger fabric of the Revolution. They measured themselves—their own purposes and the worth of their lives—by the demanding standard of the success or failure of the nation. For this reason, the young men of 1776 keenly feared that the Revolution would be lost or misconstrued by their successors. Jefferson, Adams, and their comrades chorused: What will become of revolutionary history? They merged their sense of self into their view of the nation and then judged the nation by their own ideals, works, and sacrifices.

Given the submersion of personality into public works among this revolutionary generation, it is not surprising that the maturation of these men had a visible effect on the development of American ideas. Applying modern concepts of life cycle to their thoughts should reveal patterns of motivation and response among them which went deeper than immediate commitment to policy and party. Through the prism of personal growth and adjustment, partisan pronouncements appear more cohesive and urgent; they merge with the search for self-worth, self-respect, and meaning in life and work.

The generation of 1776 matured at a time in history when one outlet for individual growth was nation-building. They seized the opportunity. As Erik Erikson has written, there are

8

moments in history when the struggle to be an adult creatively merges into larger events: "A historical period may (as for example the American revolution did), present a singular chance for a collective renewal which opens up unlimited identities for those who, by a combination of unruliness, giftedness, and competence, represent a new leadership, a new elite, and new types, rising to dominance in a new people."[9] Let me metaphorically expand Erikson's insight in terms of the four stages of adult life cycle. At a distance of two hundred years one can envision four overlapping stages of activity in nation-building from the crisis of the 1760s through the rise of a generation of politicians and intellectual leaders in the 1810s and 1820s who did not participate in the struggle for independence. The protests of the 1760s led to a Declaration of Independence in which revolutionary partisans celebrated the rescue of liberty and property from English corruption and tyranny. The second stage of this effort—the creation of independent republican governments—commenced even before the Declaration was signed. The search for political order and stability was soon extended from state to national government by the federal Constitution of 1787. New political combinations, led by former revolutionaries, arose to compete for power. The 1790s and 1800s were marked by fierce electoral and rhetorical combat among these party leaders. Finally, during the "second war for independence" against Britain and in the years following, the old revolutionary leadership gave way to younger men. As many observers over the past two centuries have noted, these periods in the emergence of the republic resemble the maturation of an individual. At the close of a youthful rebellion against tyrannical parents, the colonies grew into mature, independent states. The ensuing struggle to establish stable politics at the local, state, and national levels closely paralleled the steps a young adult takes to create a family and establish a new home. The effort to reproduce oneself—to have and rear children and pass on to them the values and ideals by which one has lived—was projected upon the larger screen of national policy during debates over the French Revolution and the two-party system. Mature men and women strive to assure that their way of life will continue; the party leaders of the 1790s and 1800s were also doing this. Finally, one finds that the effort, common to all those entering old age, to reassess and restate the usefulness of their own lives animated the last years of the founders of the republic. The parallel between state-making and individual life is only metaphorical, but for the American revolutionaries who matured in the crisis, it was a metaphor rooted in deeper truth.

Readers (particularly other working historians), will demand more proof of the utility of life-cycle explanations of changing ideas then a clever metaphor. The strongest justification for psychohistory is that it can unravel riddles of motivation and expression which have resisted (or escaped notice in) conventional treatments. One example, Peter Shaw's recent work on ritual in the Revolution, tackles a riddle—the apparent chasm between the fearful warnings of the revolutionaries and the actual indignities entailed in the parliamentary regulatory acts of 1764–74. By examining the psychological uses of ritual, he unravels the puzzle.[10] I have found another compelling set of puzzles in the young revolutionaries' ideas of history. In the course of their long careers as spokesmen for the revolution and the republic, the young men of 1776 as a group issued a series of contradictory and baffling pronouncements about American history. To them history was a very important subject—perhaps the most important measure of their own and their nation's value. History was a bridge between self-valuation and participation in the world around them. History was a beloved discipline—no generation of American leaders has taken it as seriously as they did—and historical ideas can be found throughout their public and private papers. Insofar as they identified themselves as historical figures, which was their not-so-secret passion, their views of American history became a metaphor to express a deeper sense of self-esteem.[11]

Four puzzles in their attachment to history beckon to the psychohistorian and reveal their secrets to the student of life cycle. First, as very young men immersed in the teachings and tradition of "Whig" history, they nevertheless shucked the Whig connection between America and England. They alone of all the protesters declared America's historical independence—years before the Declaration of 1776. They alone among the revolutionaries violated the Whig canons of history. Why? They did not abandon the Whig tenet that all histories were comparable, however. This they affirmed, until, quite without warning, in the 1780s, they discovered that American history was without parallel. This next twist of fact they maintained in the face of older revolutionaries' objections. Young revolutionaries of every partisan stance had joined in finding American history separate and then in asserting it incomparable, for this new proud history was their story—they created the new nation. Inexplicable, then, was their abrupt decision, in the 1790s, to divide themselves into two antagonistic schools of historical interpretation. Among them, a "party of order" and a "party of liberty" arose to contest control of America's past. Their commitment to history and faith in it had not wavered; it had merely split into two streams. How can one explain, then, the sudden and harsh rejection of history that issued in later years from the aging revolutionaries? Had they abandoned their old teacher out of despair? or disillusionment? or anger?

This book argues that the turnings and contradictions in the young revolutionaries' historical ideas were not the products of momentary partisanship, caprice, or literary convention, but were part and parcel of their attempts to face the challenges of the life cycle. History was their way of expressing their struggle with each successive stage of life. The generation of 1776 grew old with the nation, and the stages of their lives conformed to the first cycle of national self-expression. As the American people groped toward independence, the young revolutionaries pronounced that American history had always been independent. In the succeeding era of state-making and constitution-writing, the maturing revolutionaries announced that American history was not comparable to other histories and thus not governed by the inexorable laws of historical decay. As national parties advanced to do battle with each other in the 1790s and 1800s, each striving to pass on its own version of the legacy of the Revolution, the fully mature revolutionaries sundered American history into two rival chronicles, teaching very disparate lessons. When, in the years of relative partisan peace after the War of 1812, Americans sought to heal party wounds with patriotic nationalism, the aged revolutionaries once more examined American history. In moving valedictories, they pronounced judgment on it and, by so doing, upon their own labors as well. Their careers were now history, and they weighed history's verdict—in reality their own achievements—with solemnity.

Colleagues who have read this manuscript have invariably asked: Why historical ideas? Why not study ideas of republicanism, justice, law, the family, religion, or even youth and old age? The young men of 1776 are not noted for their own historical scholarship. My answers are three. First, their conception of history went far beyond the content of chronicles. In their public and private historical discourses, they touched on philosophy, government, law, family, religion, and, yes, even youth and old age. History was a way of thinking for them, not just a body of information. My account adopts their broad usage. Second, they loved history as they did not love other sets of ideas. Their passion for reading, discussing, collecting, and writing history (some of it abysmally poor) amply documents their feelings and makes possible a study of the present sort. Finally, and most important, they were a generation who preened themselves in history's mirror, conscious always of the figures they would cut in the eyes of future generations. History was a metaphor for their lives, a reflector of their aspirations and identity. History was not the only such measure, but of all of them it was the most sensitively attuned to the deeper rhythms of their lives. Political ideas (or at least political expressions) were too easily shifted by everyday currents; religious ideas were too ingrained and too conventionally expressed from childhood; but through their ideas of history we see the changing vision they held of the republic. These dreams were projections of their own sense of purpose—a fusion of personal experience in revolutionary statecraft and larger, more distant ideals of common good.

It is this last quality in the revolutionary generation—their sense of history, their yearning for fame, their will to form themselves into models of republican virtue—which makes the study of their psychological growth so important for later generations of Americans. To be sure, their day-to-day opinions and attitudes were governed no less by bias and chance than are our opinions today. The imperatives of public affairs and private ambition often motivated their conduct. But they had the unique opportunity to leave the impress of their dreams and aspirations upon the face of all subsequent American history. In their capacity to raise themselves to a temporal and spatial realm beyond their own, to lift themselves above the mundane demands of public life to visions of the broader goals of human society, they transformed their passage through life's stages into lasting structures. Put in other terms, the revolutionaries' intertwining of personal experience and public service—of their history and our history—enhanced both their lives and our own.

CHAPTER ONE

A History All Our Own: Identity, 1763–1776

A mid the turbulence of the 1760s, a group of articulate, youthful American dissidents made a declaration of America's historical independence from Great Britain. Before political independence was pronounced, before anyone, including themselves, wished for independence, these men began to fashion and promulgate a new, separate history for their communities. They broke with the historical ideas of their fathers, the Whig maxims so dear to previous generations—including older leaders of colonial resistance. In his book *A Season of Youth*, Michael Kammen has explored our lingering attachment to the American Revolution as a "rite of passage." For the younger revolutionaries, it was in fact such a rite. The controversy over British imperial policy between 1761 and 1776 was the occasion for their entry into the world of political strife. To that struggle for power they brought the idealism and optimism of their youth. Edmund Randolph, a youthful protagonist in the upheaval, later recalled: "The young . . . reacted on their fathers with new opinions, new demands, and new prospects." Assigning meaning to the ideological and political currents that swirled about them, they made the discipline of history the voice of their search for identity and their idea of the independent history of America a metaphor of their public coming of age.[1]

The oldest of these young men, John Adams, was the first to survey the new historical ground. In his *A Dissertation on the Canon and the Feudal Law* (1765), prepared for the Boston press, he sharply distinguished Old World beliefs and institutions from those characteristically American. In Europe, one found "a wicked confederacy between the two systems of tyranny . . . [bishops and kings]. It seems to have been even stipulated between them that the temporal grandees should contribute every thing in their power to maintain the ascendancy of the priesthood, and the spiritual grandees in their turn should employ their ascendancy over the consciences of the people in impressing on their minds a blind implicit obedience to civil magistracy." Adams refrained from glorifying the mother country's history, for England was not exempted from this pattern. She still had bishops (active ones, if the Puritans' fears of an American episcopate were justified), and her kings still could be tyrants. Against this system of autocracy a few brave, wise men rebelled—not by raising the standard of liberty in Europe but by casting their fortunes with a new world. "It was this great struggle which peopled America. It was not religion *alone* as is commonly supposed; but it was a love of *universal liberty*, and an hatred, a dread, an horror, of the infernal confederacy, before described." Adams continued, "After their arrival here, they began their settlements, and formed their plan . . . in *direct opposition* to the *canon* and the *feudal* systems." One must not miss the significance of Adams's argument. He was separating American history from British history.[2]

As other young men joined the protest movement, they gave voice to similar visions of historical separatism. American history had made the colonies an asylum for liberty; should Britain fail, history had begun here another experiment in liberty. In 1768, James Wilson, a young immigrant from Scotland to Philadelphia, committed to paper (though not yet to print) a historical disquisition on the independence of America. Philip Freneau, an aspiring Princeton poet, set these yearnings for a new and worthy American past to verse in 1771:

> But what change is here!—
> What arts arise! What towns and capitals!
> Our forefathers came from Europe's hostile shores
>   to these abodes,
> Here to enjoy a liberty in faith,
> Secure from tyranny and base control.
> And found new shores, and Sylvan settlements
> New Governments (their wealth unenvied yet),
> Were formed on liberty and nature's plan.
> Paradise anew, shall flourish.

Freneau's message was clear: one need only note that the "forefathers" he praised were not conceived as English settlers but as the founders of new communities, historical originals.[3] Continuing British impositions gave urgency to the younger revolutionaries' irreversible historical separatism. Even the youngest of the generation of 1776, Alexander Hamilton, made his debut in the pamphlet wars carrying the banner of an independent American history. No sooner was the slight, graceful youth of seventeen enrolled in the King's College of New York than he rushed to answer the Loyalist contentions of the New York "Farmer" (actually Anglican cleric Samuel Seabury). In his replies, Hamilton condemned "old parchments" and "musty records." Although he found the history of England and America linked at many points, the links were coordinate, not sub- and superordinate. For his purposes, American history was every bit as important as English history in establishing the colonists' right to political freedom.[4]

In the most ringing historical disquisition of all, lines that would make him the penman of the Revolution, young Thomas

Jefferson placed the case for American rights entirely upon the wilderness shore of the Atlantic. The natural rights philosophy in his *Summary View of the Rights of British America* (1774) borrowed abstractions from the Old World but drew force from use of American history. The settlers had conquered the continent not as agents of the crown but as independent entrepreneurs: "For themselves they fought, for themselves they conquered, and for themselves alone." Americans had political rights not as Englishmen, petitioning the king for a portion of their inheritance, but as a "free people, claiming their rights as derived from the laws of nature." In 1775, Jefferson drafted a declaration of the causes of taking up arms which asserted that the settlers had "established civil societies with various forms of constitutions (but possessing all what is inherent in all), the full and perfect powers of legislation." The people of Virginia constituted a political community with a history separate from that of England, based upon their own authority and law.[5]

Jefferson and his youthful allies had arrived at an unexpected conclusion: American history was not a continuation or recapitulation of English history. Whig political theory had rested upon a different Anglo-American historical concept—a concept of continuity. The "British constitution" which the older American dissidents of the 1760s—for example, James Otis, Jr., Daniel Dulany, and John Dickinson—lauded was rooted in English history. According to the canons of Anglo-American Whig history, colonists' full partnership in English history conferred English liberties upon Americans. With justice, the young revolutionaries' decision to sever these historical ties may be called novel. Although the idea of an independent American history was not without precedent in the colonies—Puritan divines long had spoken of the special destiny of their communities—the young men who fabricated the separatist history of the 1760s and early 1770s were not the inheritors of Puritan biblical typology. Many of these youths were not conventionally religious, and all of them regarded political questions as secular matters. The forces they discerned behind events were human, not divine, and their narratives focused on human acts, not divine omens. Indeed, their historical ideas derived from a materialistic, scientific culture, an empire of reason and human resources, incomprehensible without its close ties to English thought and theory.[6]

The Whig scholarly tradition embraced a liberty based on "English ideas and English principles." The young patriots often spoke of themselves as the full possessors of the privileges of Englishmen, despite the colonial status of their communities. "They knew the origins and the history of the rights to which they so persuasively laid claim," H. Trevor Colbourn has written. Anglo-American history—not separatist history—ought then to have been their intellectual home until other considerations forced them to abandon it. Nevertheless, in the years before independence, they voluntarily set forth upon the journey to a new, autonomous history.[7]

Admittedly, within the Whig tradition, history was often regarded as no more than a method of arguing from concrete examples. If the commitment to an independent American history by the young men of the Revolution was incidental to their condemnation of things English, then their separatist history might be regarded as a rationalization, adversarial points to deny English authority in America. Following this line of reasoning one could expect some older revolutionary leaders to anticipate or at least embrace quickly the concept of a separate American history. This did not occur. While just as vehement in their protests against England, the older generation of American rebels did not espouse the theory of an independent American past until after 1776. Mature revolutionaries clung instead to Anglo-American history, or provincial history, as one may term such chronicles when Americans wrote them, because it was the language of their political apprenticeship. The younger revolutionaries mastered politics under different circumstances and used history in a different fashion. They did not discard other histories—merely uncoupled American history from them. The variation is striking.

The theme that dominated the historical essays of provincial Americans was balance. The *summum bonum* of provincial culture was equilibrium between English authority and American autonomy. The great expositors of this ideal on the eve of the crisis, Thomas Hutchinson of Massachusetts and William Smith, Jr., of New York, were well into their adulthood. They became Loyalists because they could not accept an America without the harmony and order which such balance brought—a harmony and balance they had learned to accept. In the preface to the first volume of his *History of Massachusetts* (1754), Hutchinson conceived the empire as a partnership: "The addition of wealth and power to Great Britain in consequence of this first immigration of our ancestors exceeds all expectation. They left their mother country with the strongest assurance that they and their posterity would enjoy the privileges of free and natural born English subjects. May the wealth and power of Britain increase in proportion to the increase of her colonies. May these privileges never be abused; may they be preserved inviolate to the latest posterity."[8] Combined—balanced—in Hutchinson were the themes of autonomy and dependence. Smith's *History of New York* warned that upsetting the balance would bring dire consequences to the crown: "For though his Majesty has no other subjects upon whose loyalty he can more firmly depend, yet an abhorence of persecution under any of its appearances is so deeply rooted in the people of this plantation that no attempt will probably be made upon the rights of conscience without endangering the public repose."[9]

An ear sympathetic to the larger goals of such Loyalists as Hutchinson and Smith will hear much in common between their vision of Anglo-American liberty and that of earlier generations of colonists. All drew from the same traditions of provincial writing. Protest against imperial injustices regularly appeared in provincial histories—Hutchinson and Smith both voiced such concerns at one or another time in their careers. The provincial chronicler slipped criticism into a philosophical aside, as in William Penn's secretary James Logan's assurance that the colonies would be "loyal" so long as they were "treated with tenderness and humanity and not considered only as slavishly subservient to the interest of the country they come from." Other provincial historians camouflaged protest with dull technical discourse. William Keith, governor of Pennsylvania in the 1720s, reminded British readers that "we shall find, that in the advancement and security of a free commerce is the only solid foundation whereon to raise the interest, power and dignity of any state." A more rancorous critic of imperial conduct, Dr. William Douglass of Boston, cried out in 1748: "I may be allowed to drop a tear . . . over the languishing state of . . . Massachusetts Bay, formerly the glory of our plantations, but now reduced to extreme misery and distress," but he added that his purpose was to warn against "innovations upon the established constitution of our colonies." His virulent attacks upon governors and admirals, policemen and politicians, were never a prelude to separatist history. Benjamin Franklin, whose intellectual fertility had provincial roots, was a master of the hidden protest, an alchemist in alloys of optimism and good sense, practicality and material incentive. He loved the empire but was willing to chastise its rulers for past abuses: "But how contemptibly soever these gentlemen [in England] may talk of the colonies, how cheap soever they may hold their assemblies, or how insignificant the planters and traders who compose them, truth will be truth, and principle, principle notwithstanding." When Franklin demanded the colonists' due in the 1750s, he meant the rights of Englishmen in the framework of the British constitution. Protest was normal, within the accepted, conventional boundaries of greater loyalty to the empire and the British constitution.[10]

It was this carefully circumscribed, balanced form of history that older protesters advanced in their pamphlets during the crisis of 1763–66. Dissent was couched in terms of rights won at Runnymede and Marston Moor and liberties expressed in the Magna Carta and the Act of Settlement. Such Whig stalwarts as Richard Bland, Jr. (who was born in 1710) could not convince themselves to abandon the resources of the British constitution. They agreed that "we must recur to the civil constitution of *England*, and from thence deduce and ascertain the rights and privileges of the people." Such deduction might lead to strong stands against Parliament and crown, but not to a new history. When James Otis, Jr., forty years old in 1765, "deduced" the rights of the colonies, he claimed much more autonomy than actually lay in imperial precedent, but, rehearsing the supremacy of Parliament at great length, he never left British history behind. Older pamphleteers of protest held up past American sacrifices and toils with pride and decried the negligence of crown or Parliament, but they assumed that Americans had acted for Britain and deserved to be compensated for their labor. Even Patrick Henry, no stranger to historical hyperbole, saw little need for the separation of American history from English history. In 1775, at the age of thirty-nine, he consistently adopted historical rhetoric that was Anglo-American, and in private conversation he admitted that "men would never revolt against their ancient rulers, while they enjoyed peace and plenty."[11]

As the crisis worsened, the older leaders of American resistance confronted the poverty of traditional protest against Parliament. English history led not to the autonomy of the colonies but the supremacy of Parliament. Nevertheless, committed by experience and fidelity to provincial ideals, the older delegates to the first Continental Congress clung to

Anglo-American historical arguments. From such Loyalists as Joseph Galloway this attitude might be expected, but it was also true of a future supporter of independence, the mature (forty-two years old in 1774) Richard Henry Lee. Early in the first session, Lee offered a "fourfold foundation" for the political opposition to the crown based "on nature, on the British constitution, on our charters, and on universal usage." Though his subject was politics, he would not abandon the old history, at least not yet. As Lee was aware, it had become increasingly difficult to base the protests on the English constitution because the protests challenged the very basis of the constitution's applicability in America. Nevertheless, as a child of the provincial synthesis, his own identity was tied to a larger imperial connection, and for him it was not easily severed. The voices raised against provincial history at the Congress were younger and belonged to men who had come of age in the crisis era. John Jay of New York, for example, retorted "I can't think the British constitution inseparably attached to the person of every subject." He later continued that "the only authority over the colonists" was that derived from the contractual agreement of the first settlers—a separate people—with the crown.[12]

Resistance to Great Britain did not require the creation of a separate American history, and the older revolutionaries, schooled in the historical writing of the provincial period, did not hazard such a course. Instead, younger revolutionaries sounded the call for a new American history, which older revolutionaries heard and finally adopted as the official creed of the movement. The older leadership accepted the new historical vision because it pointed the way out of a cul-de-sac in Anglo-American history: there was no legitimate appeal, within the history of the imperial system, from king in Parliament. And if the colonists wished to place themselves under the king (for they lived in that legal fiction called his "ancient domain"), then they must bow to his instructions. A separate history—a history that began with their flight from tyranny, tied them to crown and Parliament only by their own consent, and left them autonomous—was a history that supported the claims of right against tyranny, including the right to rebel.

Although the younger revolutionaries advocated the separation of American and English history almost as soon as they burst upon the political scene, they did not demand (or envision) actual independence for the colonies until late in the crisis. Both Adams and Jefferson, for example, believed reconciliation to be possible and desirable through the winter of 1775. The sequence of their ideas—the demand for a severing of historical ties long before a hesitant espousal of independence—suggests that the young rebels' historical pronouncements were not propaganda for political independence. The implications of this fact are worth pursuing. The young men of 1776 went to some trouble to fabricate (an appropriate word, for their history was deliberately manufactured for the occasion) a separatist view of history but did not desire to follow the practical implications of their own ideas. The younger protesters must at first have aimed at a different target than independence. They insisted that their goal was recognition of the rights of Americans. They also sought recognition of themselves as a new generation of spokesmen for the colonies. Their purpose was at the same time greater and less than independence: a striving for identity, in which their new vision of American history worked upon two levels. The first level was public and brought them and their ideas before revolutionary councils; the second was intensely personal and attached their own fortunes, as new men, to the fate of the protest movements.[13]

It was the young who yearned for a new history, for it is the young who need a new history. Their existence—their identity and uniqueness as individuals—cannot be derived from examination of old histories. To Hugh Henry Brackenridge, then an undergraduate at Princeton, it seemed as though "'Tis but the morning of the world with us." So it might appear, for youth is a state of suspended animation, no longer childhood and not yet full maturity, at least maturity that others recognize and respect. The young person wants and needs to be someone different from others, including himself as a child. Strong emotional currents swirl through this period of adjustment and adaptation. The struggle within the individual may become violent, for it involves the rejection of childhood and the authorities who govern a child's life. A second theme of this stage of life is alienation, denial, and rejection. This can be fruitful, for it is against the authority of parents and surrogate parental figures that the youth must battle to establish identity. There is also a demand for unity of experience, for "allness" and wholeness in life. The youth attempts to pull together fragments of new and old experience, to create a new person. The challenge of identity may be postponed or partially overcome, but if it is to be met fully and successfully, the young person must assemble the materials for an integrated, adaptive personality. An individual may be more and less conscious of these strivings, but those who recognize the challenge and deal with it truly fuse their psychological needs with the larger social concerns of their world.[14]

Although today one associates the search for identity with adolescence, this was not the case in preindustrial societies. Martin Luther did not resolve this challenge until his thirties. There are sound demographic reasons to argue that all forms of maturation took place later in life in centuries before our own. Dependence upon the family, particularly upon patriarchal, authoritarian families, and the control that such families had over their children, lasted longer in the eighteenth century than they do today. Education and courtship were more disciplined, giving less scope to the early development of identity. This does not mean that the early modern Western youth did not experience the pains of the transition from childhood to adulthood. There was such a period, filled with the *sturm-und-drang* of alienation and rebellion, the search for wholeness and uniqueness, and visions of universes of possibilities. One finds the telltale evidence of such struggles in ministers' warnings against too worldly a late adolescence, tutors' protests against their collegiate charges' rowdiness, and parental condemnation of the sins of youth. These excesses were often far more fearsome to authority figures than dangerous to the youth—for what may have seemed disobedience to those above was often the young striving for identity. One may therefore posit an extended period of identity crisis for the young men of the Revolution, from their late teens until their middle twenties and perhaps beyond.[15]

The concept of identity crisis offers a new perspective upon the role of the young revolutionaries in the uprising. Historical separation from Great Britain may be viewed as an expression of the search for a separate, worthwhile identity by young men caught in a period of great stress for themselves and great danger for their society. This combination of personal needs and larger public problems provided the dynamic for the declaration of American historical independence before the 1776 document was composed. Other generations of young colonials faced similar identity crises, but in no other period of colonial history did their communities simultaneously strive so openly for self-definition and mature political status. As the personal became the political for these youths, so their own need for independence merged into their colonies' drive for autonomy.

This wedding of private life and public concerns was predictable. In the eighteenth-century American colonies, making one's way into adulthood was for the ambitious, able, propertied youth of the upper and middle classes synonymous with entering public life at some level. Civil duty and political participation were enjoined upon able young men, and many youths fulfilled these obligations. Young southern revolutionaries such as Charles Cotesworth Pinckney and Edward Rutledge obeyed the call "in which all private considerations were to yield to the public good" while still in their teens. John Adams's recollections of personal turning points in his youthful diary were invariably triggered by political events in which he had a part. For the young men of the Revolution, personal development and political causes were linked in everyday life. Even if young people from this milieu did not seek office, they kept abreast of political news, supported and often knew candidates, and sought or secured favors from government. Their rise to emotional adulthood was at one and the same time a personal rite of passage and a political event, a transition from private to public life which the entire community witnessed.[16]

There were many ways in which young men could express their hopes and fears as they made this passage. For those entering public life in the tumultuous 1760s and 1770s, a struggle against the tyranny of an autocratic father figure must have seemed inviting. They could act out, in the public arena, their need for identity, wholeness, and power—without violating the social norms of their real parents. They could seek personal identity in the drive for American identity. The very same language that clergymen and parents had used to denounce the private licentiousness of youth, the Loyalists adopted to describe the young revolutionaries' aims. The rebels were naughty schoolchildren, Anglican priest Myles Cooper of New York wrote at the height of the prewar disorders: cavorting while the teacher's back was turned, they "cabal, harrangue, resolve, rebel, associate, [and] run away." Although this Loyalist thesis had its roots in the assumption of hierarchical relationships in families, including political families, one must not dismiss the insight out of the hand. There was much groping for personal meaning and expression of youthful alienation and negation in the young revolutionaries' declarations.[17]

Were the young men of 1776 experiencing a period of identity crisis, in which the controversy with Great Britain came
to play a major, creative role, and did visions of a new history
help them to face the crisis? Before the end of the French and
Indian War, while still in his twenties, John Adams confided
to his diary that he sought fame above all else. A sincere
Puritan, he struggled with pride daily, indulging his intellect
and curbing his acerbic passion for ideas by diving into the
theoretical depths of every subject he studied. Though married and a lawyer of growing reputation in 1765, his thirtieth
year, he was still young and eager in his ambition for public
notice. He soothed ambition with applications of Puritan
homily but burned all the while with the desire to command
attention. In one arena his personal goal and his Puritan convictions coincided: in the published admonition, the scholarly
newspaper article and pamphlet on political morality, a road
to greatness lay open to him. His dissertation on the canon
and feudal law was an "old style" sermon brought up-to-
date. With it, and the stream of essays and letters on historical
subjects that followed, he became a public man. Henceforth,
his identity lay in the advocacy of the great cause of the people,
and history was his voice.[18]

On the opposite end of the spectrum of age lies a second
example of identity crisis and historical revision. In 1773,
Hamilton introduced himself to the Presbyterian elite of Eliz-
abethtown, New Jersey. Newly arrived from his mother's home
in the Virgin Islands, he was but sixteen years old. With pol-
ish and presence of mind he insinuated himself into the good
graces of Elias Boudinot and others, patrons who would help
him to the next step in his career—admission to King's College. Though without family or means, Hamilton was as ambitious as Adams and far more aggressive. Avid, confident,
and quick, the youthful undergraduate soon sat at the feet of
New York's leading Whigs. With other young men climbing
the same ladder (from a position many rungs higher than his

own), he found the crisis a source of energy and opportunity. In it, he could test his powers and, by so doing, bring himself to the attention of and receive assistance from established political figures. He would soon cast off the role of revolutionary writer for that of revolutionary soldier, but his identity was secured by his pen and the vision of a new history it proclaimed.[19]

Jefferson has left perhaps the fullest evidence of the connection between the coming of age of a young revolutionary and his need for a new history. Like Adams's, Jefferson's was a delayed identity crisis. He had taken a seat in the House of Burgesses in 1769, an aspiring lawyer, accomplished scholar, amateur scientist, a man of intellectual passions. His idealistic faith in simple republicanism and liberty—a radical faith in an age still dominated by status and wealth—had not yet burst forth. His budding legal practice and inherited lands provided a reasonable income, to which marriage to a vivacious young widow would bring additional wealth. His upcountry ways were quaint but no longer uncommon in the corridors of Williamsburg's brick houses. To others, he seemed a man of promise, and from within he was driven by the same yearning as Adams and Hamilton: he wanted recognition. When he joined the revolutionary cadre, well into his twenties, his study of history and his pronouncements on the past combined personal feelings with public opinions. He criticized the older Virginia legislators, whose minds "were circumscribed within narrow limits, by an habitual belief that it was our duty to be subordinate to the mother country in all matters of government." As protest mounted in other colonies, "not thinking our old and leading members [of Burgesses] up to the point of forwardness and zeal which the times required," Jefferson met with a number of other young men to plot rebellion. "A new generation had grown up," unwilling to submit to British authority. Jefferson, with results we have already seen, led the search into history to prove this new generation was the legitimate expositor of American rights. By one account, Jefferson's personal life had come to a crisis in these years, and his advocacy of rebellion against Britain was a release from his struggle against maternal control. One may, if one chooses to follow the parental imagery of the Declaration of Independence closely, trace his movement back and forth between resentment against parental restraints placed on him and on the colonies as a whole. It suffices for our purposes to recognize the way Jefferson resolved delayed personal identity conflicts of whatever nature with an appeal to a new American history. With "all the zeal and enthusiasm which belonged to [our] age," as John Marshall put other young planters' conversion to revolutionary activism, these men fashioned an independent history of America.[20]

Adams, Hamilton, and Jefferson were typical of this generation. For these young men, history was both the trusted teacher of politics and the vehicle by which they might gain esteem in public arenas. With the aid of historical pamphlets, letters, and essays, the last course in a graduate school of public service, the young men traversed the path from private youthful concerns to adult political responsibilities. Entry into politics had presumed an apprenticeship in ideas long before this generation arrived on the scene. The young men of the Revolution were thoroughly schooled in the utility of historical studies before they went into the wider world of affairs. Some, like Jefferson and Adams, kept careful records of their historical inquiries, following the principle that every endeavor must improve the individual as well as his society. To Adams, the study of history was worthwhile because it allowed the student to distinguish and to pursue that which was useful; it taught the lessons of real life. Jefferson insisted that history contributed "to the information of all those concerned in the administration of government." History, to

29

Adams, Jefferson, and others would remain an essential link between private and public life, spanning the two in the most virtuous way.[21]

Certain historical terms, actually formulaic references to a "new history" or a "rising empire," became for these young men a conventional medium to announce conversion to the revolutionary cause. One case in point: Timothy Pickering returned to Salem from Harvard in 1763, a gangling, uncertain youth of eighteen years. For the next decade, while he sought a wife and a career, he vacillated between Loyalism and Whig opposition. When at last he chose the revolutionary cause, he reached for a historical formula to express his decision. His future direction—his adult loyalties—determined, he portrayed himself as one of the founders of "a new empire." His radical audience easily decoded the message; Pickering had cast his lot with them. Mastery of these new historical conventions was recognized as a passport to revolutionary political prominence. With this in mind, James Madison advised his college classmate William Bradford to study history: for it seems "to be of the most universal benefit to men of sense and taste in every post and must certainly be of great use to youth in settling the principles and refining the judgment." So it was, Bradford replied, as he took up his books. James Wilson carefully polished his shelved 1768 disquisition on the historical rights of the colonies and presented it in his debut before the 1774 Pennsylvania Provincial Congress—realizing that his burgeoning political career might rest upon the reception his address received. He was correct; his reputation among the revolutionaries gained ground when his remarks circulated. Alexander Hamilton, though but two years in the mainland colonies and only a King's College freshman, sallied forth against the Loyalist pamphlets of Samuel Seabury, firing historical broadsides as he went. Elbridge Gerry of Marblehead, Massachusetts, though a Harvard graduate and nearly out of his twenties by the time that

General Thomas Gage entered Boston, also found an adult identity in the struggle against the crown and explained his rite of passage in historical terms. He might live in his father's house, remain unmarried, and work with his older brothers in the family business, but in the Whig protest against Parliament he played an independent, mature role. He gave this role larger meaning by arguing before local meetings and writing to Sam Adams in Boston that the American "people" were a different sort of men from those who ruled and were ruled in England. Americans had learned rationality and virtue in the New World, qualities that distinguished them from Englishmen. It was a difference between "we" and "they" deeply rooted in American history.[22]

Differences between "we" and "they" underlying the different historical traditions of America and England became particularly apparent to young American students in London during the crisis. Charles Cotesworth Pinckney reported how he gloried in the role of an American when news of the Stamp Act protests in South Carolina reached the imperial capital. More thoughtful responses to these events brought similar results. While studying medicine in Edinburgh, Benjamin Rush gradually discovered that Americanism and republicanism fit together. He kept his revelation to himself, but his new receptivity linked a growing sense of personal independence to an aroused concern for American interests. He began to read history, and shortly after his return to Philadelphia, he encouraged Thomas Paine to circulate his own radical views of history. Rush liked the notions of *Common Sense*, which at its center was a plea for the sovereignty of American history. Not long after Rush sponsored Paine's polemical history, the physician assumed his first revolutionary political office.[23]

Not all of the young men of the Revolution liberated themselves from tyrannical kings and more immediate parental authority by indulging in historical flights, but many did turn to history—American history—to understand their own sit-

uation. When they did, they found the notion of independence attractive, for it met personal as well as political needs.
One finds striking resemblances between the substance of
their historical essays and the characteristic concerns of youth
in the identity crisis. First, out of the many pieces of their
experience they built a new composite. Fragments of Roman
and Greek annals, of Saxon chronicle and later European narrative, were pasted together with colonial events to explain
the settlers' experiences and expectations. Remarkable cata-
logs of historical precedents, willy-nilly, in John Adams's notes
for his speech on the Quebec bill before the first Continental
Congress—"Romish religion/Feudal Government . . . Goths
and Vandals—overthrew the Roman Empire. Danger to us
all. An house on fire"—went into pronouncements on the
American historical experience. But all roads led to the present, in an egocentric quest for a larger meaning to the rebellion. These historical pastiches were not just decorative to the
young rebels, nor, as we have seen, were they a residue of
Whig historical lessons. Their significance for their fabricators
lay in an entirely different mental space. To the young men
of the Revolution, non-American historical episodes and
maxims were the whirling debris of the Whig historical universe which the crisis had exploded. Unaffected by contradic-
tion, the young revolutionaries rearranged the pieces and
added new ones of their own. Strive as later historians might
to make full sense of the revolutionaries' jumble of Saxon
laws and anti-common-law pronouncements, appeals to the
Magna Carta and denunciations of aristocracy, and countless
other contradictions, they remain evidence of the youthful
origin of the first independent history. The eclecticism of the
young revolutionaries' separatist history was produced in part
by the haste and zeal of its makers, but more important, it
was a sign of their capacity to build their own world from
portions of old and new experience.[24]

The historical separatism of these young men was filled

with alienation and anger. Freneau, poet laureate of the Whig Clio-Sophic—Clio, of course, the Greek muse of history—society at Princeton whose number included Madison and Brackenridge, swore: "Rage gives me wings and boldly prompts me on." Historical study counseled those promptings, and this in 1770, when older, wiser men still sought compromise. The king had betrayed his children, leaving them to fend for themselves at the outset of colonization and oppressing them as they grew toward maturity. The anger the younger rebels displayed here might, in some measure, have originated deep within their own guilt at rising up against an anointed king and his legitimate government. This was still a patriarchal age, and the king was the head of the family. Some felt anxiety at their disobedience, which may or may not have amounted to patricide in their minds, but could not express that anxiety if they were to pursue their revolutionary aims. In personal situations guilt of this nature is often replaced by anger at others for real or imagined injustices. It can be argued that until 1774, the crown had done relatively little to merit such abuse. The rejection of childhood and childhood's submission in this stage of life is often marked by a totalism—an unwillingness to compromise. In such fashion, Jefferson's indictment of George III in the second half of the Declaration of Independence hardly did justice to the subtlety of the author's mind or the reality of the king's conduct. Instead, it placed the king totally in the wrong and the American people totally in the right. That this historical brief had propaganda value cannot be denied, but its passion went far deeper than informing public opinion. Jefferson's prose boiled with inner anger and alienation.[25]

The anger and zeal of youth may be constructive, especially when harnessed to genuine struggles for liberty, for the aim of this anger is to build a new life. The creation of a new history, with themselves at its center, helped the generation of 1776 transform anger into identity. For some, it was a life belt in a sea of turmoil. Impoverished, frustrated, and unable to vent his feelings, Noah Webster found life at Yale difficult. The Revolution gave him a cause; he would be its prophet and interpreter. Alienated from his father and family, he found, in American history, the traits of honest and dogged virtue that his father had pressed upon him. From his first *Primer* and *Essays*, every lesson he offered the public would be couched in historical narrative. As hostile as other young rebels were to authority, they depended upon their past, their child-hoods, for identity models. The moral fervor with which the young revolutionaries wrote their histories, the sterling moral qualities they assigned to the settlers, their "forefathers," were in reality the very values parents, ministers, and teachers had demanded from every generation of colonial youth. With righteousness borrowed in this fashion from parents and teachers, the young men of the Revolution could justify their attacks on illegitimate authority—corrupt father-king and mother country. Their histories, shaped by their incorpora-tion of parental models, told them that good men had to struggle for liberty if they wished to preserve it. Whatever disorder the young rebels might have to condone, whatever destruction of property they might allow, was justified by history—their own, made into their nation's.[26]

In their drive to bring wholeness to their own experience, to give themselves an identity in this chronology of strife, they homogenized the historical variety of colonization and imperial relations into simple categories and telescoped one hundred and fifty years of colonial growth into what seemed to be no more than a generation. When Adams took up his pen to warn against the importation of bishops, he could have delved into the difference between the first New England Pu-ritan churches and the Anglican establishment of the mother country. Cotton Mather had done just that, continuing the older English confrontation between dissenters and Episco-palians. But Adams did not want to ground his *Dissertation* in the connections between England's and New England's histories. He wished instead to distance American history from its English roots. Jefferson's *Summary View* did not attempt to distinguish the variety of reasons that brought the settlers to the English colonies. He idealized and generalized the motives for colonization because he wished to portray the character of future Americans as being very different from that of their English brethren. His emphasis upon the common rights of the immigrants reduced very complex events to simple lessons. In this way, Adams and Jefferson manipulated the past to root their own vigor and virtue in earlier generations. They made American history into *their* history; its independence from parents (that is, from king and empire) was theirs; its wholeness was theirs, and they gloried in it.[27]

This young man's new history celebrated the new and the young—befitting the ambitions of men newly established in their identity as builders of a nation. "Getting forward," as Brackenridge put it, meant more than finding clients for his new law practice—it entailed establishing an empire in the wilderness. The young revolutionaries did not hunger for a provincial reputation. They wanted an identity separate from England, yet one as large and worthy as they thought the empire might once have been. The American settlements were not great—but might the purpose and promise of the young men of 1776 not be omens of future greatness? Their own grandiose estimates of the North American colonies' role in the history of liberty reassured the young revolutionaries that the future was theirs. America was the "asylum" nature provided for her worthiest refugees. Benjamin Rush boasted that "from its remote and unconnected situation with the rest of the globe [the asylum] might have remained a secret for ages" (the great importance of the British Empire would confute his argument, so he ignored the colonial status of the American settlements), but "British oppressions" gave notice to the world that the Americans would not tolerate tyranny. The rebellious colonies were now to be the center of the universe. All eyes would turn to America; all people would remember what happened there. As Adams wrote to his wife Abigail on the eve of the Fourth of July, 1776, "Yesterday, the greatest question was decided, which ever was debated in America, and a greater, perhaps, never was nor will be decided among men." Hyperbole, from a man given to caution, makes sense when the subject is the identity he had struggled to build for over a decade. Destiny spoke to these men through their new vision of history and heralded an entirely new age for men—a limitless universe of possibilities. They could, if they read the message of their own historical discovery properly, change the world in a fashion that no men had before.[28]

The recognition of the power that came with independence attracted these young men. All of them were ambitious, and independence offered the capacity to be one's own person and determine one's own future. With this goal in mind, the young revolutionaries transformed the notion of "genius" in American history. They took a concept expressing the inspiration of places and transformed it into a concept of individual brilliance. The original meaning of "genius" derives from the Latin for the protecting spirit of a particular place. Though genius might be evil or good, it always had special powers. In 1774, William Bradford told Madison, "Liberty . . . is the genius of Pennsylvania, and its inhabitants think and act with a freedom unknown [elsewhere]." The revolutionaries at first believed the New World conferred this power upon its settlers. As they explored their newly created history, they began to use a recently developed second meaning for the term. Genius came to denote the transforming brilliance of mind of an individual or group, the power that intellect and insight conferred upon men such as themselves. Bradford came upon this definition later in the year and extolled the "genius" of the revolutionary poet Hugh Brackenridge. David Humphreys, a Yale classmate of Webster, extolled the "genius" of the revolutionary leaders in a series of poems begun when peace gave him the opportunity to take up his pen. The revolutionaries had transferred the power of the Latin "genii" from external, supernatural forces to visible, internal, human agents. The young revolutionaries knew where this genius could be found; one had only to look within their own councils. The "genius" of their constitutions would become their watchword.[29]

The history they wrote and believed true was for these young revolutionaries not simply the history of the colonies but increasingly their own story. It was their heritage and their deeds, fashioned into a basis for an adult identity. Their true parents were not king and empire but the fathers of the settlements. Having chosen their parentage, they could assert freely their true identity: they were the defenders of liberty, of revolution, and finally, of republican independence. Henceforth, the history of America would truly be their history, and its glories, monuments of their identity. By separating American history from the history of Great Britain and its empire, the young men meant to leave the field clearer for the recording of their own deeds. As yet, these feats were few, but were they not mighty in significance? So Adams believed, and John Jay predicted when he told a disgruntled patriot general, Alexander McDougall, "posterity, you know, always does justice." The desire for fame, a very real part of the universe of possibilities a young man envisions, permeated the historical ideas of the young men of the Revolution. The urge was passive—a willingness to be judged, and active—a hunger for glory and honor. Douglass Adair has captured this passion: "As the war for independence enlarges the provincial stage upon which they act their roles to that of a world theatre, the greatest of the great generation develop an almost obessive desire for fame. They become fantastically concerned with posterity's judgment of their behavior." Confident of their revolutionary identity and of their adult responsibilities, the young revolutionaries welcomed the challenges of nation-building. The desire for fame, flickering in their drive for identity, burst forth in their resolution of who they were. It became, to follow Adair, "a dynamic element in the historical process; it rejects the static, complacent urge in the human heart to merely be and invites a strenuous effort to *become*—to become a person and force in history larger than the ordinary." History, their golden bridge from the passive studies of youth to the active political life, their spokesman for identity, would also lead them to greatness.[30]

The frank recognition of their potential role in history marked the way to a successful resolution of the young revolutionaries' identity crisis. The young men of the Revolution impressed that identity upon the face of reality. They drew from the history they had created before 1776 the materials for new political systems after 1776 and thereby mastered the challenge of identity as few generations have throughout history. In effect, they refashioned their communities in their own new, adult image. The independent states required the energy and confidence of youth and were founded upon forms of representative government that youth had embraced in the crisis period. The young men who operated these new governments had achieved a sense of ego integration, an "accrued confidence" in the inner wholeness and the continuity of their experiences. Placing themselves within the history that they built, they became the inheritors of the protorepublican traditions their forefathers were supposed to have enunciated.[31]

Out of the fusion of personal and public needs, each reinforcing the other, would come the substance of a national identity, the mirror of the young revolutionaries' quest for personal independence. A sense of nationhood is nothing more or less than a shared identity, an awareness of communal purposes and expectations. The rise of American nationalism has perplexed historians for two centuries. Americans were held together before 1776 by common ties to England. When these ties were severed, the only sure bond among the colonies was animosity against England. Regional and local infighting at the Continental Congresses was hardly proof of national feeling; quite the contrary. Even the first separatist histories of America, born in the crisis of the 1760s, were as wedded to locality as they were to native aims. Yet behind regional partisanships lay the great shared experience of building communities in the wilderness and defending those communities against aggressors—the fact of actually becoming independent. The young revolutionaries drew upon the reality of the very recent American past to fabricate a national history. They recognized, beneath the details of local difference, a common character and desire in all the colonies as they leaped toward liberty. If the young revolutionaries' nationalism lay not in the reality of a shared history before 1776, it could be found in these men's shared effort to define American identity, a common wish for a new kind of nation, based upon their own newly confirmed identity.[32]

CHAPTER TWO

A History without Parallel: Intimacy, 1776–1789

Even as they proclaimed American history independent of Britain's, the young men of the Revolution persisted in traditional historical comparisons. They saw their efforts in universal terms and used other countries' experiences to explain their own aims and goals. After all, the comparability of nations' histories had been a basic tenet of Whig theory. American Whig ideologues, all of them children of the Englightenment, believed that laws governed human relations no less than natural phenomena. History was the teacher of these ordinances from which men might draw useful lessons. The study of all history was applicable to any one nation's political councils, for all societies passed through the same stages, in accord with the immutable laws of political life. The rise and fall of republics was one of these tenets. Taken on its face, this philosophy of history doomed the new republic to eventual decline and dissolution; it was only a matter of time.[1]

The real world in which these revolutionaries made their way presented more immediate and practical dilemmas of survival. Between 1776 and 1789, the maturing revolutionaries faced the challenge of creating both public and private

stability in the midst of turmoil. The problem of public disorder loomed menacingly. Congress was a microcosm of discord in the nation: could a Virginian be truly intimate with a
Massachusetts man? Could delegates from large states work
with delegates from small ones? In the new states, the problem was the same: could planters and merchants, western-
country representatives and city folk join in larger communities, sacrificing self-interest to common interest? Could (and
should) the poor and rich sit down together as allies? The
conflict between intimacy and isolation, central in the young
adulthood of an individual, was written large in the nation;
localism wrestled against cosmopolitanism, East against West,
and debtor against creditor.[2]

Individual revolutionaries in the first years of maturity faced
disorder of a more personal sort. A number of domestic decisions had to be made. Would they marry? and rear children?
travel? enter a profession? give time and energy to community life? The fabrication of interpersonal relationships requires private adjustments, the most important of which is
abandonment of the consuming egocentrism of youth. Cooperation requires openness and warmth, a willingness to
give and receive. The ability to live with others marks the full
transition from youth to maturity, the end of a period of "nov-
ice" adulthood. For the young men of the Revolution, such
decisions must have been difficult. The war's uncertainty and
destructiveness, added to wearying service in the patriot cause,
imperiled courtship and temporarily dislocated friendships.
Career prospects in the law, the church, and other professions
varied under forces that the young men could hardly control.
Even if they were physically untouched by the war, the scenes
of civil strife all around them contraverted sentiments of domesticity and community. Who could tell the fate of the country, much less of a particular career or relationship?[3]

In their public stations, the young men of 1776 were haunted
by the iron laws of Whig history—the certain knowledge that,

in some future time, their experiment in republican self-government must end in failure, as all others before it had ended in failure. Whig historical maxims weighed upon them like Jacob Marley's chains. None of them escaped the burden. John Jay, then in Madrid, pleaded to an American friend: "Your irregular and violent popular proceedings and resolutions against the tories hurt us in Europe. We are puzzled to answer the question, how it happens that, if there be settled governments in America, the people of towns and districts should take upon themselves to legislate. . . . The newspapers in Europe are filled with exaggerated accounts of the want of moderation, union, order, and government which they say prevails in our country." From correspondence with political leaders in the United States, Jay knew that a dread of public immorality and political uncertainty was also spreading at home. Edward Rutledge of South Carolina wrote to Jay in 1786, "Every attempt to restrain licentiousness or give efficacy to government is charged audaciously on the real advocates for freedom as an attack upon liberty." John Marshall, at a distance of half a century, recalled the "deep solicitude" the young revolutionaries felt for the domestic political institutions of their new states. The need for political intimacy did not know ideological boundaries. In old age, Jefferson also remembered the Confederation period with regret because the uncertainty and weakness of national government endangered the great experiment in republicanism. For all but a handful of the new nation's young leaders, Gordon Wood has written, "revolutionary ideals seemed to be breeding the sources of their own miscarriage."[4]

The cold hand of the Whig theory of the past was felt particularly heavily in the councils of the new republics. Delegates to the New York State Constitutional Convention in 1777 and to the Massachusetts Constitutional Conventions that met periodically throughout the period 1776–80 divided over the form for the executive and upper house because these men remembered the injuries done to the colonies by an unbridled monarchy and an aristocratic House of Lords. If American history was determined by the same laws that had ultimately led to the corruption of the English crown and Parliament, then the power of American governors and senators must be severely limited. But could the new states survive without an energetic executive and a secure senate? The wreckage of the Articles of Confederation government and Pennsylvania voters' abandonment of a revolutionary committee system in favor of a strong executive and a longer tenure for senators gave evidence that these questions could not be avoided.

In the face of the young revolutionaries' yearning for stability and harmony flew evidence of discord from earlier American history. No colonial settlement escaped disturbances. Young revolutionary scholars had preached to the world the virtues of life in the colonies but could not still their own doubts. John Adams extolled the rationality of Americans, David Ramsay the coolness of their deliberations, and Benjamin Rush the cooperativeness of their efforts, but each of these men knew well the fury of partisanship and self-interest in the politics of the new nation. Their knowledge and their fears were widely shared by their revolutionary comrades. Self-congratulatory historical propaganda might serve the revolutionary party in time of crisis but could not dupe the revolutionaries themselves.[5]

Still trusting in the lessons of history but greatly disquieted by evidence that American history conformed to the law of decay set out in Whig treatises, several young revolutionaries commenced detailed exploration of the histories of the new states. David Ramsay of Philadelphia and Charleston was the first of these. Ramsay had relocated himself in the wake of the Revolution, moving to establish a career and family in a congenial professional setting. His mobility was typical of young adults then, as it is now, in this country. With a vision sharpened by his own search for domestic order, he came to recognize fully the imperfections in the community spirit, harmony, and cooperativeness than ran through American life. History told him and his generation that Americans had not always valued domestic harmony—at home or in their local government. After the peace treaty of 1783, Ramsay took some time to explore these disturbing historical facts. His two-volume *History of the Revolution of South Carolina from a British Province to an Independent State* (1784–85) recognized the weaknesses in the first Carolinians' attempts to build a state in the wilderness. Disease ravaged the coastal plantations much of the growing season, and the upland woods, filled with lurking savages, hardly offered a safe haven for the "weary and heavy-laden, the wretched and unfortunate of Europe." The emigrants, products of varying national backgrounds, had difficulty living in harmony. Domestic, religious, and political contention, as well as constant warfare on the frontier, disrupted the colony. British supervision maintained a semblance of law, but even when Britain ruled justly and generously, "everything in South Carolina contributed to nourish the spirit of liberty and independence . . . its settlements were nearly coeval with the [Glorious] Revolution in England, and many of its inhabitants had imbibed a large portion of that spirit . . . every inhabitant was, or easily might be a freeholder, settled on lands of his own, he was both farmer and landlord. Having no superiors to whom he was obliged to look up, . . . he soon became independent." Independence meant not only republican liberty but also a continuation of the license and disorder of the past. Ramsay, who had served in the 1782–83 session of the Confederation Congress and would go on to high office in South Carolina, knew that these conclusions could be extended to all the new states. In February 1786, shortly after finishing his *History*, Ramsay mourned to Benjamin Rush: "In 1775 there was more patriotism in a village than is now in the 13 states." Such a decline in republican civic virtue was foretold in Whig history, as

Ramsay, from his wide reading, well knew. It presaged the death of republics.[6]

If proof was needed of the dangers inherent in native American disorderliness, the years after the peace of 1783 brought abundant evidence: the controversies over the state constitutions, the struggles of creditors and debtors for control of state government, and, above all, a rebellion in western Massachusetts. When Daniel Shays led western Massachusetts farmers against the state, younger revolutionaries concerned with newly won public harmony decried renewal of revolutionary disorder. History told of the mortal dangers of insurrection. If former rebel captains like Shays could turn upon a state that had led in the Revolution, what republican government was safe from endless private dissatisfactions leading to countless public uprisings? Caught in the middle of a lecture tour by the uprising, Noah Webster found his utopian revolutionary hopes dashed. Safe again in tranquil Connecticut, he decided, "Nothing can be so fatal to morals and the peace of society, as violent shock given to public opinion or fixed habits." Aghast at the prospect of political upheaval coming to New Haven, Humphreys insisted that the "discipline, and the institutions and examples" of past generations of orderly patriots must be impressed upon their unruly descendants. Humphreys helped to script a mock epic, the *Anarchiad*, which grandiloquently blended real fears of disorder with rhymed bluster at Shays's defeat by the government. The poets truly conceived themselves with guardians of the "temple of liberty" and were petrified by the specter of rabble in arms.[7]

Granting the danger was real, one wonders why the young poets were so troubled. They had urged revolution and war but ten years before. They had learned insurrection at its source. Why, now, did they feel such fear of disorder? Humphreys was fast becoming a mournful prophet of political and social conservatism, but a yearning for order was not confined to conservatives. From the opposite side of the political spectrum came murmurings of a similar timbre. In 1787 Humphreys invited his Yale classmate, Joel Barlow, to deliver the Fourth of July address to the Hartford branch of the Society of the Cincinnati. Barlow was a reformer and would soon be a radical Francophile, but his *Oration* restated Humphreys's poetry: "The existence of our empire depends upon the united efforts of an extensive and divided people." Isolation, diffusion of purpose, and antagonisms among Americans were Barlow's targets.[8]

As the desire for intimacy bridged differences in political ideology, so it spanned discord over particular laws and policies of government. Though, in the heat of rebellion, many a young revolutionary may have demanded the death of the "father-king," all of them placed "tranquillity" and "due supremacy" high on their lists of constitutional priorities. Whatever the forms of their fundamental laws, they conceded to their new governments the power to make binding statutes and to punish offenders. The most radical of the young men of 1776 did not object to the creation of criminal courts with powers of life and death, nor did the most conservative of them prevent almost all of the states from the unheard-of novelty of bills or declarations of rights. Lifted to office by their revolutionary comrades, such exponents of liberty as Jefferson were just as decorous and law-abiding in their tenure as conservatives Fisher Ames and Rufus King. If, behind all these young men in their new posts surged the will of an aroused people, they regarded themselves as its trustees. Poles apart in their particular goals for government, Jefferson and Hamilton labored to make government more efficient and orderly. Schooled in different philosophies of social growth, Webster and Freneau both begged young Americans to put aside private gains and serve the public interest.[9]

The young revolutionaries' need for order was more basic than ideology or political preference. Disorder was not the opposite of tradition for them; it was the enemy of intimacy. Would-be reformers and future conservatives alike were robbed of prospects by disorder. Barlow could not write his poems, nor Webster sell his books, in times of rebellion. Local rebellions disrupted careers barely begun and threatened future hopes. The common fears of young revolutionaries can be illustrated by comparing these men with their older comrades. The young often felt disorder in a different way from the older revolutionaries, a difference of perspective growing out of a difference in stage of life. To take one example, Edmund Randolph and George Washington, adoptive son and figurative father after Randolph's biological father elected to remain loyal to the crown, corresponded frequently about the state of national affairs. Both men lamented corruption in government, self-seeking among officials, and popular unrest. Both were galvanized to action by Shays's rebellion. But the disorder meant something very different to the two because of the difference in their stages of life. Washington watched with dismay from Mount Vernon, his public career (so far as he could have predicted) at an end. He urged reform and then joined in it because of his concern, which Randolph himself would grasp as he grew older, to preserve and secure his life's labors. The younger man had begun a splendid political career as attorney general and would shortly be governor but was still seeking to make a lasting contribution to his country. He looked to the future, and from his office in Richmond, his view of the crisis was more pained and anxious than Washington's. Young men of Randolph's generation saw disorder as an immediate problem, which could not be ignored. Randolph's fears were vivid and personal: "The nerves of government are unstrung, both in energy and money, and the fashion of the day is to calumniate. . . . What then, am I to expect?" he wrote to Washington upon his election to the Virginia governorship. Washington's fears were just as genuine but less immediate: "As no mind can be more deeply

47

impressed than mine is with the awful situation of our affairs
. . . so, consequently, those who do engage in the important
business of removing these defects, will carry with them every
good wish of mine."[10]

The need for order so keenly felt and widely shared among
the generation of 1776 bridged the public and the private
spheres. Disruption in politics intruded directly upon the lives
of the politicians in this generation. The weakness of the Confederation government drew the young revolutionary leaders away from their newly established families to sit in
assemblies and congresses. Jefferson, frantic with worry over
his sick, pregnant wife, periodically scurried home from the
House of Burgesses in Richmond. Bachelor Elbridge Gerry
could not choose between affairs of state and the attraction of
a lovely young fiancée. After years of indecision, he elected
to marry and settle in Cambridge but continued to find politics too irresistible to abandon entirely. In March 1789, James
Madison received a letter from Charles Cotesworth Pinckney
explaining that Pinckney could have had a United States Senate seat, but with a wife about to deliver a child, an ailing
mother, and a big new house, he had decided to remain at
home. For all his plaintive cries, Pinckney had already served
his state and his country at the cost of domestic harmony. His
service was typical of his generation. Though sentiment turned
their thoughts toward home, the younger revolutionary politicians did not abandon public life. They arrived at adulthood in the midst of political crisis and created a basis for
adult life in their protest writing and their revolutionary committee work. They hoped aloud that their efforts to ensure
national harmony would lead to true domestic peace. Typically, Hamilton, though he left the Continental Congress and
"retreated into domesticity"—law practice and family life in
New York City—nevertheless used the respite from public
office to plan for a new federalism. Troubled by the chaos left
by the war, surrounded by more disruption than they ever

cared to see, the young revolutionaries strove all the harder for constitutional order and political stability.[11]

For other young men of 1776, isolation and economic depression were more terrifying than public unrest. Men of talent and ambition lamented the isolation of much of the western portion of the country. Brackenridge wailed that his "solitary residence" in western Pennsylvania drove him to despair. He did not fit in with the roughnecks and hayseeds. Who did? Not Freneau, who found Philadelphia and Charleston filled with unruly mobs and bloated speculators. Nor Webster, whose single-mindedness sustained him in temporary jobs, as he peddled his speller and his vision of a new language. But these men, as Madison and Jefferson, bore the stamp of the revolutionary experience upon their very features. They first took up their pens to defend rebellion and independence, and they still found their future prospects in the success of the republic. Scratching for a living at the end of the war, Joel Barlow admitted, "I am yet at a loss for an employment for life," but was buoyed by his faith that "the American republic is a fine theatre for the display of merit of every kind. If ever virtue is to be rewarded, it is in America." Webster, at work on his speller, agreed: "It is the business of Americans to select the wisdom of all nations . . . to add superior dignity to this infant Empire and to human nature." He pledged to work toward that end.[12]

The parallel between the young revolutionaries' search for domestic stability and professional advancement for themselves and the young nation's search for political and constitutional harmony is not farfetched or metaphorical. The young men saw its validity. As quick as they were to perceive the tie between independence and their own coming of age, so they grasped that their domestic arrangements and future prospects were indissolubly bound to the success of the American experiment. Contemporaries were well aware of the complex intertwining of personal and public commitments in these critical years. When Rufus King of Massachusetts married a New York merchant's daughter, John Jay was quick to commend King for breaking the barriers between states, and John Adams, whose daughter had also wed a "Yorker," solemnly declared to King, "It will be unnatural if federal purposes are not answered by all these intermarriages."[13]

Committed by private convictions to the public good, indeed, identifying their future with that of the republic, the generation of 1776 anticipated the fatal verdict of Whig history all the more keenly. If all republics were governed by the same laws of birth, growth, decline, and decay, if American history were no exception to the iron law of dissolution, what use were the young men's efforts? For them, it was no distant, abstract theory but the corporeal prophet of disaster. As it doomed the republic, so it doomed them; as it threatened harmony in their councils, so it portended discord and dissolution in their homes. The argument of Whig history must be refuted, not just to complete the intellectual edifice of American republican thought but to give the generation of 1776 peace of mind. In the arenas of politics in which some of them would congregate, they championed a variety of practical solutions to the dilemma posed by Whig history. All of them, future federalists and future antifederalists, recognized the imperative of finding an answer to the dire forecast of the laws of history.

As the tie in their lives and minds between the fate of the republic and their own prospects brought them to this agonizing pass, so it also pointed a way to refute the iron law of republican decay. If American history were incomparable— unlike any other—then it would not be fated to recapitulate the dismal past record of republics. The generation of 1776 probed this logic early in the 1780s. In the midst of the disorders they saw about them and those they cataloged from earlier American experience, the young men of 1776 began to see a hopeful pattern. Americans had proved that they were an enlightened people, a people willing and able to compromise, cooperate, and reason together to solve common problems. Looking at history from this new perspective, a vantage point to which their search for harmony carried them, they discovered—like Barlow's "Columbus"—an empire of reason. The disorders were real (and predictable, according to the Whig canon), but the capacity to settle disputes and create legitimate, representative government was also real—and, these men asserted, unparalleled. The Whig laws thus did not apply here. The young revolutionaries of 1776 already had shown that they did not consider received historical wisdom to be sacred. History was their tool, to be refashioned for each new task. They had done just that in the crisis before the Declaration, motivated by the combination of personal and public striving for identity. Revising their view of history once again, they pointed the way toward a new national stability. They found in America's experience evidence of true intimacy: shared aspirations, effective local governments, and self-sacrifice for the common good. This discovery proved American history incomparable to that of other republics and, at the same time, rationalized the dynamics of constitutional reform. It placed control of events in men's hands and took them out of the realm of an unfavorable, discomforting natural law.

The new vision of American history also had its price: the incomparability of American history, the basis for a national community, seemed to divorce events here from those elsewhere in the world. To ensure their future, the young had to yield part of their claim to leadership in world renovation. One must remember that the young men of the Revolution had already sworn to the world that American history and the history of other oppressed peoples was linked. These revolutionaries offered themselves as proof that no people need remain the vassals of another, or of kings and nobles. It would not be easy to cast off this mantle of universalism, for it had been worn proudly and sincerely. Nevertheless, the need for domestic harmony was more compelling than promises made to foreigners in a time of peril, and the maturing revolutionaries followed this intellectual course, convoluted as it was. Ramsay's apologia was typical: "I am a citizen of the world, and therefore despise national reflections; and hope I am not inconsistent, when I express my ardent wish that Law, Physic, and Divinity may be administered to my country by its own sons." From all points of the ideological compass, the generation of 1776 approached this nationalistic solution to the problem of domestic intimacy. Among them, the young federalists would join the youngest antifederalists in the discovery. With a new vision of history to guide them, the generation of 1776 would chart a novel American constitutional course, isolating American experience in their journey toward cooperation at home.[14]

Hints of the young revolutionaries' discovery of the incomparability of American history multiplied throughout the 1780s. Their commitment to historical universalism remained strong but could not resist the growing pressure of exclusivistic nationalism. Rather than formulate an immediate synthesis of moral universalism and empirical isolation (which would come, a generation later, in the work of George Bancroft and others), the revolutionaries vacillated between the old and the new historical formulas. In 1787 Timothy Dwight beheld a vision of an unprecedented history, a republic that descended from "the skies," though in earlier poems he had sorrowed at Americans' inability to cast off the wants and weaknesses that plagued earlier civilizations. Other revolutionaries of his generation were still ambivalent in their feelings and unsure of their ground. Joel Barlow made his poetic persona "Columbus" promise, with true revolutionary universalism: "No more the noble patriotic mind, to narrow views and local laws confined." The same Columbus also saw an empire to end all empires in the New World: "Each orient realm, the former pride of earth, where men and science drew their ancient birth, shall soon behold, on this enlightened coast, their fame transcended and their glory lost." To the Hartford members of the Cincinnati he made the conclusion more specific: the American Revolution succeeded because "on the western continent the scene was entirely different [from anywhere else], and a new task, entirely unknown to the legislators of other nations, was imposed upon the fathers of the American Empire." Benjamin Rush called for the teaching of all kinds of history, to show "the progress of liberty and tyranny in the different states of Europe." Nevertheless, above all he wished American history taught, for the "true principles of republics," as he told Jeremy Belknap, could not be discerned in the experiences of America's predecessors: "Mankind have hitherto treated republican forms of government as divines now treat the doctrine of final restitution. Both had been condemned before an appeal had been made to experiments, for both have been accused of leading to disorder and licentiousness." By rejecting the authority of Enlightenment commentators on republicanism, Rush was pledging himself to the new, incomparable American history.[15]

American history could provide a basis for future progress and tranquillity only if it were severed from other nations' past experiences. The logical consequence was that the history of the American Revolution could no longer be assumed to be the forerunner of world renovation—a model, yes, but no longer a precursor and partner. Such historical observations as Barlow's and Rush's, if not an unconditional withdrawal of American commitment to universal revolution, were frank statements of the priority of domestic harmony over global reformism—and this from two future defenders of the French Revolution.

The two fullest and most self-conscious explorations of the incomparability of American history, Jefferson's *Notes on the State of Virginia* (1781–86) and Adams's *Defense of the Constitu-*

53

tions of . . . the United States (1787–88), were produced by men of different political persuasions—but common determination to escape the trap of Whig laws of decay. Both addressed European audiences on the issue most pressing to their generation. The *Notes* and the *Defense* were less retractions of earlier promises of support for world revolution (Jefferson never really recanted this pledge, and Adams never really made it) so much as *apologiae* for the discovery of the uniqueness of American constitutional experience. The *Notes* began in 1781, as an answer to a French inquiry about life in the new states. Jefferson admitted that "in every government on earth there is some trace of human weakness, some germ of corruption and degeneracy which cunning will discover." This was a good Whig maxim, but Jefferson found indications in the history of the colony that Virginia government and law were unique. The people of that community had never bowed to tyranny, believed imposture, or accepted the status quo. The moving force behind the constitutional progress of the state was its people's continuing role in making and running government. The people understood "[The constitution] pretends to no higher authority than the ordinances of that same session; it does not say it shall be perpetual, that it be unalterable." In the mixture of genuine popular sovereignty and constitutional reform lay the basis for a community unlike that seen anywhere before. Woven through this period of his life was Jefferson's struggle for domestic peace of mind. Perhaps, if he could not claim exemption from the laws of chance that cost him his wife, he could augur a better fate for his state.[16]

Adams, like Jefferson, had found a unique historical cement for American political materials. The United States were different from other nations, he opined, because they were wiser. Adams's chief work of this period, the three-volume *Defense of the Constitutions of . . . the United States*, was culled from many continental sources—typical of Whig comparative history—but undercut the Whig thesis, for its moving force was his own effort to draft a constitution for Massachusetts that would surmount the difficulties of its European predecessors. How was this possible? From his first paragraphs, in volume 1, Adams boldly preached the virtues of America's enlightened representative government. He began with the general premise that "the arts and sciences in general, during the three or four last centuries, have had a regular course of progressive improvement," but he emphasized that only in America, where the general population had excelled in the Whig "science of politics," were the lessons of experience wisely employed. All the settlers understood and protected their old civil liberty. "The people [of the colonies] were too enlightened to be imposed upon by artifice, and their leaders, or more properly followers, were men of too much honor to attempt it." A foundation thereby existed in shared institutional experience for balanced government, and, consequently, "The United States of America have exhibited perhaps the firmest examples of government directed on the simple principles of nature; and if men are sufficiently enlightened to disabuse themselves of artifice, imposture, hypocrisy, and superstition, they will consider [the American Revolution] as an era in their history." Even as he penned these encomiums to American constitutionalism (and his own Massachusetts document) his optimism was severely shaken by Shays's rebellion. Though he was never again to expect so much, so easily, from his country, he never foreswore his underlying faith in its incomparable preparation for its special mission of republicanism.[17]

Barlow and Rush were ambivalent; Jefferson and Adams clung to Whig precepts even as they hurled Whig "laws" overboard; but all had discerned that American institutions would survive the constitutional crises of the 1770s and 1780s and surmount unknown crises to come if and only if the new republic was historically unique. Only then would the United

States not be bound by the laws that doomed other republics. The recognition of the need to make American history incomparable, to isolate the American experiment from foreign antecedents, was tied to no particular view of political reform. It was instead a product of a new maturity in the revolutionary generation: a drive to uncover the possibility of intimacy beneath the disorderly surface of the confederation. Even Hamilton, who had no illusions about the superiority of American character, readily conceded that "it is ridiculous to seek for models in the simple ages of Greece and Rome" to refashion American institutions.[18]

At the Constitutional Convention, which met in Philadelphia in the spring and summer of 1787, Whig comparative history was tested against the most immediate and pressing needs of American politics and found wanting. At first, young and old delegates turned for political wisdom to the history of other peoples. During the early weeks of the convention, James Madison often referred to ancient councils and the Belgic and Helvetic Confederations, and Wilson tried to draw lessons from Persia and the Roman Empire. Yet these references no longer were convincing, and Wilson admitted that "if a proper model was not to be found in other confederacies—it was not to be wondered at. The number of them was small and the duration of some at least short." In these circumstances, it was logical and astute of the federalists among the generation of 1776 to attempt to establish their new view of American history as the orthodoxy of federalism. The preparation of a federal system was the solution these young men of the Revolution assayed to the problem of intimacy, and into it the notion of an unparalleled history fit perfectly. Madison, the leader of the young federalists, announced that a serious detriment existed in the use of examples from the histories of other nations. On June 21, he told the convention: "All the examples of other confederacies proved the great tendency in such systems to a disobedience of the members." He argued that this, and not "a tendency to a tyranny . . . of the federal heads," was the prospective fate of the American confederation. But if all other attempts at confederated government had ended ruinously, and Madison admitted they had, there was only one chance for America's success. Madison found it to be in "the character of liberality, which had been professed in all the constitutions and publications of America." American history, with its "representative principle" and its "enlightened people," was different from the history of the Old World. As Charles Cotesworth Pinckney put it, "The people of this country are not only very different from the inhabitants of any state we are acquainted with in the modern world, but I assert their situation is distinct from either the people of Greece or Rome, or any of any state we are acquainted with among the antients." Pinckney's implication was clear: Americans should use their own past as the source of political instruction. The other young men of the Revolution at the convention agreed.[19]

The logic of history was now on their side: a new federal system, unseen in other nations' histories, could be conceived and would be successful in America because American history was unparalleled. The appeal of this dual revelation about American history and the federal Constitution was irresistible. In state after state, public debate on the Constitution, climaxing in the state ratification conventions, proved that American history was fast being accepted as unique and superior by federalist and antifederalist. The younger federalists wasted no time employing their idea of a unique American history to support the proposed Constitution. Noah Webster wrote a pamphlet for the Connecticut ratification convention in which he "showered the architects of the new government with praise . . . [for] this western world now beholds an era important beyond conception . . . the names of those men who have digested a system of constitutions for the American empire, will be enrolled with those . . . collected by posterity with the honors which *less enlightened nations* have paid to the fabled demi-gods of antiquity" (my italics). Webster extolled the American Constitution as an advance over all previous forms of confederated government: "In the formation of our constitution, the wisdom of all ages is collected, the legislators of antiquity are consulted, as well as the opinions and interests of the millions who are concerned. In short, it is an empire of reason." Such an accolade to American reason was common in the federalist publications and echoed their use of American history during the Philadelphia convention. As Webster put it, "Experience is the best instructor—it is better than a thousand theories . . . but I appeal only to American experience." Webster then compared the new American Constitution to its two most respected predecessors, the Roman and the English. He found the American document incomparably superior because it truly embodied the popular will. Webster believed American reason, incorporated into the federal system, would guarantee the continuing excellence of the new Constitution—just as it would Americanize the English language.[20]

Another younger revolutionary turned federalist who found the Constitution a product of America's special historical virtues was New York Chief Justice John Jay. In his addresses to the people of that state on the proposed Constitution, he wrote that the escape from the old European historical cycle of loose confederation, followed by political dissolution, lay in the careful reading of the lessons of American history. The proper model, according to Jay, was the American Revolution: "The people answered 'Let us unite our counsels and our arms.' . . . Confiding in the probity and wisdom of Congress, they received their recommendations as if they had been laws." The events of 1775 and after had "proven the wisdom" of listening to America's political leaders when they called for a strong federal congress. The representatives of the people,

JOHN ADAMS
1735–1826

1766   1783

1793   1823

Top left: Portrait by Benjamin Blythe, Massachusetts Historical Society. *Top right:* Detail of a portrait by John Singleton Copley, Harvard University Portrait Collection. *Bottom left:* Portrait by John Trumbull, Harvard University Portrait Collection. *Bottom right:* Copy by Gilbert Stuart (1826) of a portrait he painted in 1823, National Museum of American Art, Smithsonian Institution.

THOMAS JEFFERSON
1743–1826

1786

1791

1805

1821

Top left: Engraving by Timothy House (ca. 1884) of a portrait by Mather Brown. *Top right:* Portrait by Charles Willson Peale, Independence National Park Collection. *Bottom left:* Portrait by Gilbert Stuart, National Gallery of Art. *Bottom right:* Portrait by Thomas Sully, American Philosophical Society.

JAMES MADISON
1751–1836

1783   Ca. 1805–1807

1817   1833

Top left: Miniature by Charles Willson Peale, Library of Congress. *Top right:* Portrait by Gilbert Stuart, Mead Art Museum, Amherst College. *Bottom left:* Portrait by Joseph Wood, Virginia Historical Society. *Bottom right:* Portrait by Asher B. Durand, Library of Congress.

ALEXANDER HAMILTON
1755–1804

1777   1792

1799   1805

Top left: Miniature by Charles Willson Peale, Frick Art Reference Library and Nathaniel Burt. *Top right:* Portrait by John Trumbull, National Gallery of Art. *Bottom left:* Portrait by P. T. Weaver, Museum of the City of New York. *Bottom right:* Sketch by Gordon Fairman, New-York Historical Society.

according to Jay, must again recognize the vision of those same leaders.[21]

Even when the generation of 1776 resorted to Greek, Roman, and English historical arguments to support the Constitution it was to show how different America was, in temperament and experience, from those other nations. It was the thesis of *The Federalist*, for example, that America's new Constitution had remedied the defects of the older governments; in this context historical examples from Greece or Rome proved only the inadequacy of copying Greek or Roman forms of government. In scholarly pieces, Madison and Hamilton, with the assistance of Jay, presented the conventional wisdom of Whig history with this twist: they employed standard historical illustrations in a negative sense, to prove how superior the new American Constitution was to the political arrangements of the other nations. One of the papers Madison and Hamilton collaborated on gives an idea of the historical tactics of *The Federalist*. The eighteenth number began a summary of the confederacies and republics of the past and found: "Among the confederacies of antiquity the most considerable was that of the Grecian republics . . . from the best accounts transmitted of these celebrated institutions, they bore [a] very instructive analogy to the present confederation of the American states." The analogy was drawn out by the authors: "The powers, like those of the present Congress, were administered by deputies appointed wholly by the cities in their political capacities. Hence the weakness, the disorders, and finally the destruction of the confederacy . . . it happens but too often, according to Plutarch, that the deputies of the strongest cities corrupted those of the weaker; and that judgment went in favor of the most powerful party." The conclusion, the point which the authors elicited from ancient history, was that America was different from the older confederacies because she had the capacity to make an unparalleled improvement upon the ancient constitutions. The references in *The Federalist* to the history of other nations had meaning only when its readers understood, as the authors intended, that the new American government defied comparison.[22]

A few of the young men of the Revolution opposed the Constitution as it was presented. These men had nevertheless arrived at the same general conclusions about American history as the young federalists. Elbridge Gerry, though a delegate to the convention, was not pleased with its product and campaigned against it in Massachusetts. There he published a pamphlet, *Observations on the New Constitution*, in which he reproached the federalists, "who have made the most costly sacrifices in the cause of liberty." He accused them of forgetting the lessons of British tyranny in America, "which the brave sons of America have fought with a heroism scarcely paralleled even in ancient republics." Gerry's indictment of the proponents of the new government was precisely that they, and not the antifederalists, had forgotten the bloody lesson of the American Revolution and aimed at the establishment of a new despotism. He appealed to Massachusetts voters to reject the proposed Constitution "before they are compelled to blush at their own servitude, and to turn back their languid eyes on their lost liberties."[23]

The maturing revolutionaries of 1776 on both sides of the ratification issue presented their most involved and complete historical arguments in the state ratification conventions. In each of these extraordinary gatherings, the controversy over the meaning of American history was renewed in face-to-face confrontations. The Massachusetts convention assembled in January 1788, and the first session gave an indication of the changed attitude toward and increasing attention given to American history. The very first issue considered by the delegates was the two-year term for congressmen. In Massachusetts, one-year terms for the lower house were the rule.

Theodore Sedgwick, who entered politics as a young revolutionary and had become a prominent political conservative, rose to discuss the effect of the two-year term. "It had been mentioned by some gentlemen that the introduction of tyranny into several nations had been by lengthening the duration of their parliaments," the reporter of the debates recalled, and Sedgwick wished to know "what were the nations which had been thus deprived of their liberties." He believed they were few in number. He added that he did not see how the change from a one-year to a two-year term "had any effect in *American* history" (my italics). The next day, Fisher Ames, whose political conservatism had grown strong in the days between his youthful revolutionary activity and the present debates, returned to the matter to argue for a longer term of office for elected representatives. He avowed that no evidence from "the paltry democracies of Greece or Asia minor" would convince him that a two-year term was improper. Rufus King, a young revolutionary who would later lead the Federalist party in New York, agreed that "from the continent of Europe . . . we could receive no instructions," and he would not attempt to manufacture them. But "it has been said that our ancestors never relinquished the idea of annual elections: this is an error." It was an error King attempted to correct by explicit reference to Massachusetts's political history alone.[24]

King, who had been at Philadelphia, also attempted to explain why the authors of the document had begun with the phrase: "We, the people . . . " instead of "We, the States . . . " as the convention had been instructed. Once again he turned to America's unique history to explain: "In the ancient governments, this has been the principal defect. In the United Provinces of the Netherlands, it has been conspicuously so," but "in America . . . the representative principle has ruled." Thus, "we, the states" was a preamble inappropriate "to a representative government." Another federalist, John Gorham, proposed to go further and "exposed the absurdity of

conclusions and hypotheses, drawn from ancient governments, which bore no relation to the confederacy proposed,"
for again, "those governments had no idea of representation
as we have." The youthful federalists made clear that they
intended to appeal to American history, not to examples drawn
from ancient or European history.[25]

Before the final balloting, Ames tried to rally the remaining
undecided voters to the federalist standard with the now
proven appeal of American history. He spoke to "those who
stood forth in 1775 to stand forth now; to throw aside all
interested and party views." To this plea one antifederalist
delegate retorted that he, too, had stood forth in 1775 and he
found in the present Constitution the same design as the British conspiracy of 1775: "Does it not take away all we have—
all our property." Representative John Nason of Maine summarized the antifederalists' fears of the Constitution with an
extended historical reference to American history, which was
by that stage of the debate the expected form of historical
illustration:

> When we felt the hand of British oppression upon us,
> we were so jealous of rulers, as to declare them eligible
> but for three years in six. In this constitution we forget
> this principle. . . . A standing army! Was it not with this
> that Caesar passed the *Rubicon*, and laid prostrate the
> Liberties of his country? . . . We had a Hancock, an Adams,
> and a Warren. Our sister states, too, produced a Ran-
> dolph, a Washington, a Greene, and a Montgomery, who
> led us in our way. Some of these have given up their lives
> in defence of the liberties of their country. . . . and had I
> an arm like Jove, I would hurl from the globe those vil-
> lains who would dare attempt to establish in our country,
> a standing army.

Both sides had come to draw their historical lessons from
Massachusetts and America, not from Rome or Europe or

even England. Older revolutionaries, as in 1776, came to adopt their younger colleagues' views of American history. All ages and sides had agreed that the proper aim of government was the preservation of America's unique political freedoms.[26]

In the Pennsylvania convention, James Wilson, a supporter of the proposed Constitution, made the same two points about the inapplicability of non-American historical examples to the current political crisis as were made by both the Massachusetts federalists and antifederalists. First he noted: "we were deprived of many advantages which the history and experience of other ages and countries would, in other cases, have afforded us." This was the result of the lack of proper historical works, to the end that "the facts recorded concerning their constitutions are so few and general, and their histories are so unmarked and defective, that no satisfactory information can be collected from them concerning many particular circumstances." There remained a second obstacle in that "the situation and dimensions of those confederacies, and the state of society, manners and habits in them, were so different from those of the United States, that the most correct descriptions could have supplied but a very small fund of applicable remarks." A truer lesson could be derived from the experience of the American people than from the history of any other nation.[27]

To the south, the Virginia ratification convention was marked by even fuller exploration of the nature of American history. The first sessions saw the establishment of a clear pattern: Patrick Henry, an antifederalist who had grown to intellectual maturity in the generation before Wilson, Madison, and Hamilton, opposed the Constitution with copious comparative historical references, while young federalists Robert Nicholas, Edmund Randolph, and Madison insisted upon the incomparability of American history. In traditional Whig fashion, Henry insisted that "revolutions like [ours] happened in almost every country in Europe; similar examples are to be found in ancient Greece and ancient Rome—instances of the people losing their liberty by their own carelessness and the ambition of a few." He implied that this would be the result of the adoption of the federal Constitution. Henry lamented the lost passion of America: "When the American spirit was in its youth . . . liberty, sir, was then the primary object." He even ventured the alternative of a confederation modeled upon Switzerland to the document now before them. Henry's first speech thus moved easily between American and European history, seeking in both effective replies to the federalists' case.[28]

Edmund Randolph gained the floor on the following day to dispute Henry's ideas about history. He believed Henry had been misguided in his reasoning by the use of irrelevant historical arguments, such as those he drew from the case of Switzerland: "Sir, references to history will be fatal in political reasons unless well guarded. . . . Examine the situation of [Switzerland] comparatively to us: the extent and situation of that country is totally different from ours." Randolph warned, "From the year 1776 to the present time . . . the history of the violation of the constitutions of America extends." The people of America had simply lost their respect for law. The real alternative to the proposed Constitution, Randolph suggested, was not a recreation of Switzerland's cantons in the New World but a recreation on American shores of the "perpetual scene of bloodshed and slaughter" in Europe. This above all was to be avoided.[29]

Madison was no more satisfied with Henry's use of history, especially Henry's attachment to foreign histories. Madison dismissed the example of Switzerland as "quite unworthy of our imitation" and proceeded to pinpoint the real dangers to the republic, as he saw them: "Turbulence, violence, and the abuse of power, by the majority trampling on the rights of the minority, which have produced factions and commotions which, in republics, have, more frequently than any other cause, produced despotism." Later in the session, Madison

summarized his extensive researches into the history of confederations, with different conclusions from Henry's:

> If we recur to history and review the annals of mankind,
> I undertake to say that *no instance* can be produced by the
> most learned men of any confederate government that
> will justify a continuation of the present system. . . . The
> uniform conclusion drawn from a review of ancient and
> modern confederacies is, that, instead of promoting the
> public happiness . . . they have, in every instance, been
> productive of anarchy and confusion, ineffectual for the
> preservation of harmony, and a prey to their own dissen-
> sions and foreign invasions. [My italics.]

Madison concluded that American history had in it the material for a much sounder, in fact, a unique constitution, and
no other nation's history could be cited to disprove this.[30]

Nevertheless, Henry returned to the floor to defend his
reading of Swiss history. "They have stood the shock of four
hundred years," he told his critics, "and enjoyed internal
tranquility most of that long period." Throughout the following days, he offered the political history of Holland as an
example of the evils of a strong central government. He pronounced the inordinate power of Stadholder to be the cause
of the ruin of the Dutch. Finally, he decided to appeal to the
history of Virginia, adopting the tactics of the younger federalists to prove his case. "What did the genius of Virginia
tell us? *Sell all and purchase liberty.*" He continued, "On this
awful occasion, did you want a federal government?" Virginians had not known feudalism or vassalage or tyranny, at
least for long, and thus the lessons of the failures of weak
ancient republics or modern confederacies cited by the federalists did not apply to Virginia. "We differ in this from all
countries," Richard Henry Lee, another older antifederalist
now agreed, for "our present government is well suited" for
Virginia's own needs. With the conversion of their Whig-

schooled fathers to the exclusivist concept of American history, the victory of the young federalists was inevitable.[31]

When the Constitution was ratified, all the young revolutionaries of 1776 rallied to it. Regardless of their particular interpretation of its articles, the document became the symbolic fruition of their quest for stable domestic relationships. In this situation, it was entirely appropriate (though, one must admit, also expedient) that late federalists and recent antifederalists found the Constitution, and the American experience that gave the new government its form, to be unparalleled in history. If it were circular to use the Constitution as proof of the incomparability of American history, it was neither inconsistent nor novel to place the Constitution at the apex of the long development of American institutions. At a 1788 Philadelphia Fourth of July commemoration also celebrating state ratification of the Constitution, Wilson extolled, "A people, free and enlightened, establishing and ratifying a system of government they have previously considered, examined, and approved . . . is the most distinguished spectacle that has yet appeared on our globe." Wilson was convinced of the truth of his oratory. In his later law lectures at the University of Pennsylvania, he displayed vast erudition about other nations' legal systems but persisted in the assertion that American law, derived from American history, was superior to all others.[32]

The establishment of a national government brought the fruition of domestic pursuits closer to these men. Skeptics, such as Thomas Jefferson, put aside serious reservations to serve in the new government. The once-young revolutionaries, with a few exceptions, controlled the first federal offices. In a very real way, the federal government became a home for these men, not replacing their own families but enlarging the family and projecting it upon the screen of national life. The generation of 1776 went on to dominate the first twenty years of federal policymaking. Once again, the path out of a personal life-cycle challenge for them had led to public service, aided by a new vision of the meaning of American history. Madison rested at his home between sessions of the first United States Congress, confident that the nation would now survive. The extraordinary and taxing diplomatic missions of Adams in London, Jay in Madrid, and Jefferson in Paris ended as these men returned home. Though they would all serve in federal posts, their domestic lives would never again be as irregular as they were in the 1780s. Typically, George Nicholas, who had served alongside Madison in the heady debates in the Virginia ratification convention, joyfully wrote to Madison of his resettlement in Kentucky, "following the business of a farmer and a manufacturer without any interruption but what the calls of my profession [as a lawyer] cause." Of course, true to his identity as one of the young men of 1776, he added, "Unless indeed I also add the moments I employ in trying to point out the real situation of this [frontier] country."[33]

The young men of the Revolution had solved the problem of intimacy by turning their energies inward. They promoted harmony with a federal union, permitting loyalties to state and local governments to exist untouched. By so doing, they denied themselves full participation in world revolution. Declaring friendship and commerce with all, but commitment and debt to none, they isolated America. The neutrality policies grew from, among other sources, the combination of celebratory and exclusivistic themes in the new historical nationalism. Hamilton, writing a draft of a farewell address for George Washington, went beyond his own generally cautious view of the virtues of Americans to celebrate the "magnanimous and *too novel* example of a People always guided by an exalted justice and benevolence" (my italics). Hamilton had reached for and found the central tenet of the nationalistic historical consensus of the 1780s.[34]

To be sure, American history could not be separated from

events that were to come—no American revolutionary went that far. When delegations of revolutionaries from other countries approached American leaders for direct assistance in the years after 1789, they were rewarded with sympathetic lectures on the American historical model. This they were to copy, if they could. If the American Revolution could not be directly exported (because American history was "too novel"), others might still learn from it. Wilson proposed at the end of the ratification debates: "We shall probably lay a foundation for erecting temples of liberty in every part of the earth." He told the Pennsylvania convention that its example "will induce princes, in order to preserve their subject[s], to restore to them a portion of that liberty of which they have for so many ages been deprived." Wilson and Hamilton were far more chary of foreign upheaval than Jefferson or Madison, but the latter two did little more for their French and South American supplicants than offer their own faith that revolution abroad was following the American model and deserved American goodwill.[35]

In the 1780s, the revolutionaries were maturing. The great enthusiasm of youth was falling away before the political realities of adulthood. Political uncertainties in the 1780s had accelerated the process. The contraction of revolutionary history's boundaries to the Western Hemisphere was not a cynical view so much as a considered judgment of grown men, forced to confront more immediate problems than the eventual fate of the oppressed peoples of the world. Who among them anticipated that a European revolution would explode in the very first year of the new federal government or that the French Revolution would force American revolutionaries to review the meaning of colonial independence from a new perspective? Not as youthful participants but as sober parents, the American revolutionaries would have to determine

68

if their own rebellion was complete or unfinished. As we shall see, the importunings of the French radicals for advice came at another critical time in the life cycle of the American leaders and would leave their concept of their uprising permanently altered.

CHAPTER THREE

History as Process vs. History as Order: Generativity, 1789–1815

Among the myriad responsibilities of parenthood in revolutionary America was the education of children. For the upper and middle classes, education absorbed a substantial portion of family time and resources. While private tutors and public academies flourished after the war, parents still played a visible role in setting and monitoring educational goals for their offspring. In a broader sense, transmission of the mores and values of a culture to its inheritors ensures its survival. No generation embraced this doctrine more fervently than the young men of 1776. Among them, Jefferson founded a university so that republican ideals might be inculcated among the talented young; Rush sponsored academies for women to spread the revolutionary message; Jay and Adams prepared guides for the education of American youth abroad; and Webster fabricated spellers, readers, and other educational materials for the next generation. The Revolution had stimulated "a rethinking and recasting" of the goals of education—politicizing the schools and refitting them as factories of republicanism. A new era in education was at hand, in which the generation of 1776 had a large stake.[1]

Although the results of their enthusiastic efforts at reform were not uniformly pleasing to them—riots at colleges, financial difficulties, and lingering incompetence at lower levels of instruction brought cries of dismay from the would-be reformers—the revolutionary generation continued to insist upon a national commitment to improvement and expansion of education. For Noah Webster, whose financial prospects depended upon this project, an obvious motivation was private gain. Why did the other young revolutionaries of 1776 find the need for new and better schools so compelling? Why did these otherwise busy men spend so much time and energy on educational matters? One clue is telling. During the 1770s and early 1780s education was not so high upon their list of priorities; later in their lives, it assumed far greater importance. An answer is obvious: they became much more concerned with education when they themselves became parents, particularly when their children were old enough to read. With children whose education they directed and could take pride in surrounding them, they began to examine more general educational questions. Within their sitting rooms and libraries and, when public duties separated them from family, from distant places, they prompted, guided, commended, chided, and basked in their children's educational progress.[2]

There comes a time in the life of a mature adult when the urge and opportunity to transmit personal experience and ideals dominates other interpersonal relationships. A parent is faced with the task of passing on experience. The danger is stagnation—an inability to reach, communicate, and instill one's own values in the hearts and minds of one's children, with the terrible consequence that the next generation will be unprepared to deal with the challenges it faces. The late 1780s and early 1790s found the generation of 1776 acutely sensitive to the challenge of transmitting their values to others. Their own parents were dead or retired, making the once-young men of 1776 into the heads of families and the leaders of the nation. They were now truly the "fathers" of the republic, and they bore the parental burden of ensuring that republicanism survived. The new Constitution was an expression of that yearning, and their public vows under it to "preserve and defend" federal government echoed and reinforced their roles as mature parents.[3]

As in their past personal quests for identity and intimacy, the onus of generativity for the generation of 1776 was dual. Their private strivings invariably became the motive for public activity. As they tutored their own children in the subject matter of republicanism, so they assumed the duty of rearing up a nation of young republicans. This is why they took the time to aid infant colleges and support public expenditures for schools. Again, they did not—could not—separate the private and the public.

A large measure of the educational interest of these men revolved about the discipline of history. They made history, watched themselves making history, admired themselves making history, and confidently lectured on its lessons to younger audiences. They believed that without a full understanding of American history, and the revolutionary experience at its center, the young would not be able to preserve republican liberties and institutions. "A few pieces of American history," Barlow boasted to Webster, were a far better tutor of truth than any other text. In letters that may seem stuffy today but were penned with concern and affection, Adams, Jefferson, Jay, and their comrades urged a similar course of study upon their sons and daughters. Not content with private tutorials, for their pupils were all young Americans, the generation of 1776 sponsored and engaged in public historical disquisitions. Their goal was obvious: the young must learn from the sacrifices and achievements of the old. As Ramsay wrote to Jeremy Belknap, "I wish such men [as created the Massachusetts Historical Society] could be found who would take equal pains in writing the history of each state.

We are one people in name but do not know half enough of each other . . . to cement our friendship and intercourse." Barlow insisted as he grew older that everyone, old or young, ought to go back "to the school" to learn the lessons of American history. As in previous challenges to their sense of self and their future plans, history transcended the role of rhetorical tool and tutor; it became a cry from the heart. The young men of 1776, who had first announced their full adulthood with manifestos of American historical independence, in the 1790s attempted to perpetuate the republic with historical confessions. At the end of the decade, Marshall pleaded that history, "if we value it rightly and support it firmly," would preserve the new generation from "misery, division and civil wars." They enfolded autobiography within historical discourses, for the history of the Revolution was now their history, a narrative of their works, and their greatest gift to their children.[4]

The once-young men of 1776 were not the first to face generative challenges at this stage of the life cycle. The first Puritan settlers instructed their sons and daughters in the special duties of tending the "garden in the wilderness." History has always been a part of these lessons, though the text might vary from one generation to the next. Oral history and written history are the primary transmitters of human experience. The revolutionaries' historical didacticism was not unusual, but what they did with American history in later middle age was unexpected and dramatic.

The eruption of the French Revolution put these Founding Fathers (a term that by then fit this generation) to an immediate test of pedagogic commitment in its largest sense. In 1789 and 1790, Americans could not stop their ears to the French appeal. Jefferson and Paine in France, American visitors throughout Europe, and French spokesmen in America shouted the message: France was following in American footsteps. Controversy over policy toward France among the revolutionaries of 1776 combined with the challenge of generativity to force a subterranean rift over the meaning of American experience to rise to the surface. The revolutionary generation was driven to focus upon an unresolved dilemma: was their own Revolution truly finished? In particular, was the Revolution a process—one giant step forward on the long road toward fuller equality and liberty—or was it a conservative effort to purify and guard an older order? Did transmission of republican values to a new generation of Americans depend upon further domestic revolution—more change, experiment, and reform—or did it depend upon the conservation and perfection of established institutions? The French upheaval, followed by war between France and England, made the issue unavoidable. The generation of 1776 came to believe that failure to define the limits of our Revolution would result in stagnation of republican institutions and the waste of the previous decades' effort. The choice of strategy was momentous, both from a personal and a political perspective, and under the pressure of the French controversy, the historiographical consensus of the 1780s crumbled. Factions rose to do battle over the meaning of the American past. Parties of liberty and order, as John Quincy Adams later recalled, fiercely contested disparate visions of American history. No mere scholarly difference of opinion, their struggle over historical ideas reflected the generation's attempt to grapple with the challenge of maturity, to pass on the true heritage of the Revolution to the next generation.[5]

To be sure, the ideological split over the reception of French revolutionary thought in America was not caused by the increasing maturity of the generation of 1776. Nor did historical concerns dictate how Jefferson or Adams would regard the French constitution of 1789 or the later regicide. Age, life cycle, and historical ideas fit into complex patterns of motivation. The point is that in the 1790s the stage of life of the revolutionary generation of 1776 and the demands of the French

74

radicals combined to produce an unexpected and (from the Americans' perspective) unexplored shift in their historical thinking, a shift that should not be minimized in importance. The partisan issues of the 1790s are so familiar and the urgency and energy of the protagonists so enervating that one may lose sight of the importance and novelty of the subject at hand. It is nothing less than the tearing of revolutionary historical thought into two distinct and antagonistic parts, not to be reunited in the lifetimes of these Founding Fathers. On the surface, destruction of three decades of literary and intellectual labor is surely a puzzle. During the crisis, the revolutionary war, and the years of constitution-making, the young men of the Revolution insisted that American history was a separate, unique saga, incomparable and praiseworthy. It was a versatile, appropriate thesis, for it bound together the different states and regions, as well as rationalizing the speed and violence of the Revolution. This view of history was a foundation for emotional unity and national scholarship. The 1790s witnessed the mature revolutionaries' demolition of this historical thesis, laying bare with almost compulsive ferocity the latent conflict between liberty and order in America. The historical essays of the 1790s were perhaps truer reflectors of American experience than earlier revolutionary chronicles, but the exaggeration of the two concepts of liberty and order into polar opposites was hardly a sign of rising historical realism. Instead, the twin pressures of external exigency and internal life-cycle challenge had driven the revolutionaries to ransack American history for polemical ammunition in an internecine war.

The stress placed upon the American revolutionaries by the French Revolution from without and from their own generative wishes from within does not of itself explain the bipolar fracture of national history. Why not a multitude of historical visions expressing individual revolutionaries' answers to the riddle of the preservation of the republic? Each of these men did wrestle with this issue, but any answer to the broader paradox must fit the irreducible fact that two general views did emerge and the revolutionaries joined in the task of explicating one or the other of them. Michael Kammen has posited the existence of certain "biformities" within American culture which are so pervasive and so compelling that they tended to arrange thought in a bipolar fashion. A biformity is the simultaneous presence of two intrinsically opposed ideas within the same cultural framework. The commitment to both the extension of liberty and the preservation of order in these years was such a biformity. The fragmenting of historical thought in the 1790s was influenced by the larger biformity. A split between history-as-process and history-as-order was implicit in pre-1790 historical essays, and the combined pressure of diplomatic crisis and maturational strain fell on this fault line. The revolutionary generation came to blows over this question in the 1790s because the need to hand down their political ideals, the challenge of "generativity," induced them to explore the full range of their differences over the meaning of the uprising. Their view of history (their own history and the history of the Revolution, now inextricably bound together), still the mirror of their inner lives and their struggle for full maturity, shattered along the margins of their ideological disagreements over liberty and order.[6]

In their defense of the French Revolution lay the essence of one group of mature revolutionaries' effort to nurture republicanism at home. For the achievements of the "party of liberty" to be impressed upon a new generation of Americans and stamped upon the face of the republic, the young had to be taught that American history was a process. Led by Jefferson, again the penman of their cause, these revolutionaries insisted that the American upheaval was not a discrete event, a thing in being, but a becoming: a gradual, incomplete unfolding of human potential. They characterized the American Revolution as but one major victory in a continuous, often bloody struggle against tradition, superstition, and tyranny. It was to them the central event in American history not because it concluded the search for liberty but because it typified the process of experiment and reform. From one standpoint, this argument was a self-serving retrojection of their immediate political aims back into American history, a method of giving legitimacy to their progressive policies. By expanding the American Revolution to include the entirety of American experience, these men made support for the French Revolution a test of support for true American principles. And if revolution and American history were synonymous, then the American Revolution could not be over. Had American history stopped with 1776, 1783, or 1789?—no more than in 1761 or 1774. The "party of liberty" concluded that the same forces expanding liberty in the 1760s and 1770s were grappling with English-spawned reaction in the 1790s. The real issues were change, reform, and human freedom, not France, neutrality, or regicide.

If the French Revolution was not the source of these Jeffersonians' commitment to history-as-process, it was a catalyst in the refinement of that concept. Initially, there was general enthusiasm for the French uprising. Among conservatives, advocacy soon chilled into wariness. Not so for Jefferson, Madison, Freneau, Barlow, Brackenridge, and their allies. Even a man so little given to ecstacy as Brackenridge exulted, "O! France, if thy republic perish, where is the honor due to ours?" Jefferson and Freneau were passionate men, but Brackenridge and Madison were not—why did the latter then join in perfervid displays of sympathy for France? Jefferson had aided the fledgling revolutionaries, Freneau was proud of his ancestral heritage, but Madison and Brackenridge and many more of the pro-French party did not have any contact with France. Could gratitude for French intervention in 1778 have so moved some of the generation of 1776 and not touched the rest? The commitment of these men to the cause of France drew strength from life-cycle sources. Actual aid to the French never amounted, even among these men, to more than words of praise and expressions of encouragement. Their labor was educational, not diplomatic or military, and the motive for it was kin to the motive for educating their own children. They adopted the French Revolution as their child and regarded its progress as proof of their generative powers. It became the litmus test of their capacity to transmit their own particular vision of republicanism to others. At the heart of this vision was not a set of principles which France must duplicate in order to merit American aid. Instead, they hoped that France would master the process that lay at the center of American experience (as they perceived it), the guiding principle of American history. Jefferson named it when he wrote to Madison in September 1789: "The earth belongs in usufruct to the living." Here was a principle of American history that could be exported (and did not violate the new doctrine of incomparability). The American Revolution had established this principle but did not dictate for all time the content of another nation's history, for the principle was one of process, not substance. If and only if every generation had the right to refashion its constitutions and laws, and no generation had the power or right to bind any future generation to debt, subservience, or antiquated custom, then and only then would the future be safe for liberty in that nation.[7]

To Jefferson's side in the struggle to establish that America's creative power (and their own personal generativity) lay in continuous change, reform, and progress came other members of his generation. All fused personal ideology, life-cycle promptings, and public careers in their defense of France. Madison, leading spokesman for France in the House of Representatives, explained the principle behind the historical analogy to the readers of the *National Gazette*, Freneau's pro-French newspaper. Madison reasoned: "Every nation has the right to abolish an old government and establish a new one.

This principle is not only recorded in every public archive, written in every American heart, and sealed with the blood of a host of American martyrs, but is the only lawful tenure by which the United States holds their existence as a nation." The object was to teach the French the central tenet of American history and aid them while they applied it to their case. Freneau also reminded his readers of this analogy. "The movements of human life," the editor perceived, "in all its various stations, have and forever will be responsive to the same principles, and the principle upon which the French Revolution was founded is not new here."[8]

Even when, after 1793, the French situation diverged from the Francophiles' expectations sufficiently for stalwarts of the pro-French party to admit that the course of the French Revolution would be a perilous one, Jefferson and his allies still linked their own power to teach to their continuing advocacy of reform. "We have chanced to live in an age," Jefferson wrote to a French friend in 1795, "which will probably be distinguished in history for its experiments in government on a larger scale than has yet taken place. But we shall not live to see the results." Only the time scale for renewal of reforming energies had changed. When the French republican experiment ended in Bonapartism, Jefferson maintained his faith in revolutionary change and experiment. He merely sighed to Joel Barlow, "There is a snail-paced gait for the advance of new ideas on the general mind, under which we must acquiesce."[9]

But if American history were incomparable, where was the danger in the miscarriage of the French uprising? America would still be safe. The dramatic language of the friends of France among the mature revolutionaries showed as much fear as hope. Their unease and irritability grew not from the erratic course of the French Revolution—for this they forgave or dismissed as the natural excess of Gallic enthusiasm and a necessary self-defense against aristocratic machinations. France was not their prime concern. The twistings of events in the French republic were seen as clues to the fate of the American experiment, for the obverse of the Francophiles' historical analogy made revolutionary France's troubles into a warning against dangers American republicanism might face. As Jefferson told Edmund Pendleton, "The question of war and peace is still doubtful. . . . The success of [the French Revolution] will ensure the progress of liberty in Europe *and its preservation* here" (my italics). The important question to the mature Jeffersonian revolutionaries was who or what stood in the path of continuing revolution in America.[10]

Their study of the French Revolution enabled the Jeffersonians to identify and execrate the political aims of Britain and her American friends. They accused America's English sympathizers of refusing to accept change, of turning back the clock to return the United States to subservience to Great Britain. Unregenerate Tories and English agents, the Jeffersonians averred, warped history to support a pro-British neutrality policy. In mid-1793, Freneau sounded the tocsin: "Certain persons here see nothing but castles, crowns, sceptres, lords, knights, princesses and kings." The radical editor insinuated that the friends of England wanted to reverse progress so much that they would welcome a reestablishment of medieval political and social institutions. Freneau, an able revolutionary propagandist, well knew American fears of medieval fealty to kings and priests. He was not alone in these fears. In a "Candid State of Parties" (1793) for the *National Gazette*, Madison found that Toryism still existed in America and was organizing itself in the federal government to oppose not only France but revolutionary creativity in America. Throughout his essay, Madison identified the enemies of the French Revolution with the enemies of the 1776 upheaval. During the Jay Treaty ratification debates of 1795–96, supporters of the treaty provided the friends of France with additional evidence for their claim that republicanism would languish in

Federalist hands. French sympathizer Edmund Randolph, who lost his cabinet post during the controversy, trumpeted the attack on the pro-treaty forces: "They were the enemies of France, the friends of monarchy, and the violators of our constitution." At stake in all of these contests was more than foreign policy; it was the Francophiles' capacity to sustain their procreative power. The Revolution had either to go forward or to die. Covert alliance with England was not just an erroneous policy, it was a betrayal of revolutionary principles. Submission to England denied that Jeffersonian ideals had any generative power.[11]

The mature revolutionaries who joined Jefferson in defense of continuing reform soon agreed that one guarantor of future generativity would be a national political party. The Republican party that Madison, Jefferson, and others created was to be both spiritual repository and active engine of ongoing revolution in America. The organization of a party not only would enable the inheritors of "true" revolutionary principles to exercise national power and so transmit their values to successive generations but would become a model of political generativity for younger men to emulate. Organized national party opposition to government might be almost without precedent in Anglo-American political ideology, but the Republican party, championing the rights of the oppressed and checking arbitrary power, would claim to be the voice of the people rather than a party.[12]

The formation of parties, when party activity and particularly organized party opposition to government were prohibited by longstanding maxims, expressed parental as well as partisan impulses. Hamilton's program was the initial cause of Madisonian opposition, but Madison's trek along the coast of the country in search of support and his leadership role in the first Congresses bespoke deeper commitments. Hamilton's second message on the debt, the Neutrality Proclamation, and the Jay Treaty controversy heaped fuel on the fires, but Madison tended the embers between times. The need to ensure the survival of republican principles (as he understood them) drove Madison beyond the pale of conventional antiparty wisdom. The solicitude a parent feels for a child—in this case, Madison's for his Constitution—outweighed the cold instructions of Whig political theory. Madison and Jefferson, when the latter joined in the party struggle, now occupied the position Washington held during the 1780s (and, to continue the analogy, Thomas Hutchinson and William Smith, Jr., occupied in the 1760s). They were not mere factious men but teachers, whose textbook was history and whose classroom was party.

However impelling the urge to pass on true republicanism might be to them, organized political opposition was so new that the Jeffersonian Republicans only developed a full justification of their party activities when the Alien and Sedition Acts made opposition to government liable to criminal prosecution. Republicans of the generation of 1776 responded by arguing that the Sedition Act reversed history in America. The reasons why the Federalists in Congress would pursue such a course had already been explored in earlier Francophilic essays. In their counterattack upon the Sedition Act and the Alien Acts that accompanied it, Republicans blended the idea of revolutionary history-as-process into a defense of organized political opposition. Again, this thesis was self-serving, for it gave the sanctity of revolutionary origins to an instrument of partisanship. At the same time, one must remember that in these controversies past and future were bound together for the mature Republican party leaders. It was their past that was disputed and their power to hand down their views that was challenged by the threat to the future of their party.

The Republican outcry against the Seditious Libel Act was not limited to members of the party who matured in the crisis of 1776, but their response to it arose in different headwaters from younger Republicans' sources of discontent. Republicans who had come to adulthood in the 1790s correctly saw the seditious libel law as a dagger aimed at their party's heart. Their present and future were imperiled. Older Republicans regarded the party in a different light; they remembered a time when there were no national parties. The Republican party for them was not merely a necessity of politics but an insurance policy, the end result of a struggle they began in the 1760s and 1770s. Again, they turned to history (now almost synonymous with their own historical achievements) to make this point. Republicans Edward Livingston, St. George Tucker, and George Nicholas, young men of 1776 whose aspirations and experiences were similar to those of their more illustrious comrades, dug into history (as much recollection as scholarship) to inform Americans of the meaning of the Revolution. The will of the people was then paramount. The Republican party, threatened with extinction by the seditious libel law, was the inheritor of that tradition. How could the revolutionaries transmit republicanism to a new generation, if the Republican party were to be destroyed by its enemies?[13]

Throughout 1798 and 1799, other mature Republicans echoed these sentiments. James Madison's draft for the Resolution of the Virginia House on the Alien and Sedition Acts, followed by an address to the people passed by the Virginia lawmakers in 1799, combined legal and political history to vindicate Republicanism. Madison combed colonial, revolutionary, and Confederation history to verify the fact that the common law of libel—the source of the Seditious Libel Act—was never received in any American federated government. The English law, which had "deluged the scaffold with blood," ill suited American society and government. It became the duty of the assemblies of the people to reject the common-law-derived Alien and Sedition Acts. The Republican party, the organized arm of the popular will, obeyed the living mandate of the Revolution in its opposition to Federalist rule. He concluded:

"And a fair comparison of the political doctrines not unfrequent at the present day with those which characterized the epoch of our Revolution, and which form the basis of our republican constitutions, will best determine whether the declaratory recurrence here made to those principles ought to be viewed as unseasonable and improper, or as a vigilant discharge of an important duty." That duty was the regeneration of republican values.[14]

Jefferson, who became fully engaged in the mechanics of party controversy in the early 1790s, understood the danger of the Alien and Sedition Acts and the need for a positive historical justification of opposition. The acceptance of Republicanism would establish once and for all the legitimacy of revolutionary history-as-process as a generative philosophy. Jefferson joined the campaign against the acts with his secret authorship of the provocative Kentucky Resolutions. "Free government," Jefferson thundered, "is founded in jealousy, and not in confidence; it is jealousy and not confidence which prescribes limited constitutions, to bind down those whom we are obliged to trust with power." In 1801, after his election to the presidency, a still-worried Jefferson wrote to Elbridge Gerry: "The only difference [from 1776] is that the leaders [of the Federalists] who remain behind are more numerous and bolder than the apostles of Toryism in '76." The triumphant Republican party would not reinstitute the Revolution, but with power in its hands, its members could rest assured that republican principles would be transmitted to the next generation.[15]

Needless to say, political parties advanced other ends than the transmission of accumulated personal knowledge. Party organization conferred immediate material benefits upon the victors of electoral and legislative contests. Nevertheless, even the brief view of Jeffersonian revolutionary history above suggests that beneath the ambition of the mature Jeffersonians for political advantage, there lay a shared purpose to impart a body of republican wisdom to younger inheritors of their offices. All of these advocates of the extension of liberty had reached a sobering stage of life. They were the older generation. The task of maintaining family and state fell to them. The historical lessons they offered to the nation reflected the parental demands of maturity. Embedded in their solemn invocations to the saving power of revolution was an admonition to a child: make the world better.

The historical ruminations and proclamations of the generation of Jefferson and Madison on the meaning of parties have a different quality from the "chronicles" of party that James Callender, John Daly Burk, and James Duane, to name a few of the younger party polemicists, produced. The former spoke from concern for the republic, from their teaching responsibility; the latter, able writers and hardy propagandists, merely used past events as evidence of the Federalists' shortcomings. The past was very dear to the aging Republicans; though they did not wish to stop time, its great moments were part of their lives. Younger Republicans, introduced to politics in the 1780s and 1790s, did not yet share the urge or the need to find and transmit lessons from past experience. To take one example: William Branch Giles of Virginia, thirty-six years old when the Federalists passed the dreaded Sedition Act, was as angry and afraid of its consequences as his mentor, Jefferson, and his colleague in the House, Madison, but his historical disquisition against it had none of their attachment to the past. When, more than twenty-five years later, he returned to the subject (as governor of Virginia, speaking before the assembly), his reminiscences did ring with a concern and sense of proprietorship of the past. By then, of course, he had passed into the generative stage of his own life.[16]

Mature revolutionaries who opposed Jefferson and Madison also experienced the need to transmit cherished values and ideals. Many Federalists who had worked with the two

Virginians to secure domestic tranquillity in the 1780s recoiled with horror at the politics of Republicanism. The French Revolution, praised by the Republicans as symbol (if not reality) of human striving for liberty, genuinely frightened Hamilton, Adams, Ames, and others of their persuasion. While younger Federalists pressed on with organization of the party and competition with local Republican leaders, Federalists who had matured in the crisis of 1776 had more at stake in the contest against French radicalism and its American admirers. To protect and hand down their own version of republican values was their prime objective. Despite the fervor of their condemnation of France, Adams, Hamilton, Jay, and Pickering did not fear that the United States would enter war on the French side. Even Jefferson and Madison had agreed to neutrality. The aging Federalists feared the influence of French ideas because they wished to transmit a very different body of ideas about republicanism to younger Americans. In part, this is why the animosity of the Francophobes magnified in intensity after the regicide. These men held no love for Louis, or for kings in general. French republicanism should have pleased them—but the removal of the French monarch's head made France into a true republic—and thus a rival tutor of republican decorum and authority. How could the priority of their own experience be established in the face of "Jacobin" enthusiasms? As did the Republicans, the "friends of order" turned to the trusted discipline of history to state their case to the next generation. Fisher Ames understood the root of the historical musings of his comrades in this decade: the Federalists "wish not only to enjoy but to perpetuate liberty, by giving energy enough to government to preserve its own being, when endangered by tumult and faction." Properly taught, American history would not only support current programs but ensure the preservation of the republic.[17]

The Federalists of the generation of 1776 launched a three-pronged historical campaign to transmit their view of republicanism. First, they prepared accounts of the Revolution, the writing of the Constitution, and the origins of party contest, which proved that American institutions worked because Americans were an orderly, moderate, and virtuous people. What they valued themselves they perceived in the past. Perception followed desire, for history served inner needs. The Federalists of this generation discovered the secret of the success of the Revolution in the sober character of its men and the stability of its institutions. During one partisan contest early in Washington's second administration, Timothy Pickering asserted that his party, unlike the opposition, was composed of men "of sense and experience, who gave the reins, not to . . . passions, but to reason." Fisher Ames took pleasure in recalling the origin of Federalism: among his colleagues, reason checked enthusiasm and built a stable federal government. "No sooner did the new government begin its auspicious course, than order seemed to arise out of confusion." Sensible men led the ratification effort of 1787 and strove, after 1789, to maintain sound government.[18]

Reasonable men, Ames and others explained, had built lasting public institutions from the founding of the colonies to the inauguration of President Washington. From his diplomatic post in Lisbon, David Humphreys lauded the administration for uniting energy, reason, and harmony. Humphreys credited this achievement to the fact that the government in the 1790s was staffed and directed by the same men who wrote the federal Constitution. As Gouverneur Morris reminisced in 1804, "History, the parent of political science, had told the writers of the Constitution that it was almost as vain to expect permanency from democracy as to construct a palace on the surface of the sea." Instead of the unruly mobs and demogogues of democracy, the constitution-makers of 1787 wisely created a "balanced republican government" of "sound principles." A year later Marshall combined the personal and public Federalist collections into the fifth volume of his *Life of*

George Washington. "In 1786," he wrote, "the continent was divided into two great political parties, the one of which contemplated America as a nation and labored incessantly to invest the Federal head with powers competent to the preservation of the Union. The other attached itself to the state authorities." In this crisis, "enlightened men of sound politics" gathered to support the federal Constitution in the federalist party. The antifederalist "confounded liberty with an exception from legal control . . . it was a disorderly spirit which moved them." To Chief Justice Marshall, the division over the Constitution was that between the "sound and unsound, republican and democratic, orderly and anarchistic."[19]

The second prong of the Federalists' attack was to condemn the Jeffersonians' analogy between the revolution in France and that which they had led in 1776. It is easy to understand the horror with which these aging men of "sound principles and steady habits" watched the growth of French revolutionary sympathy in the United States, for France's influence threatened the intellectual and moral bequest they intended to will their children. John Fenno's *Gazette of the United States*, the semi-official organ of Hamilton's friends, published a stream of older Federalists' essays asserting that the American Revolution was endangered by "Jacobin" intrigues. Ames worried "how far we shall probably travel in the revolutionary road and whether there is any stopping place." To leave behind the steady and sure, the orderly and sensible, was to ignore the lessons of the Revolution in America.[20]

Mature Federalists rejected all analogies between French and American history. Gouverneur Morris, after service in Paris, judged that "the French were inspired by our example," but there existed little similarity between the two revolutions: "We were in the actual enjoyment of our freedom and fought not to obtain but to secure its blessings." The French revolutionary government would inevitably deteriorate into a "despotism both in principle and in practice," because the

French "had to create a new political system" for themselves, whereas the American revolutionaries had only to "preserve their ancient and beloved" representative government. In a letter to President Washington urging a policy of neutrality, Hamilton insisted that only revolutions similar to America's merited American support. Process was not important; content was. In order to resemble the American Revolution, the French rising had to be "a free, regular and deliberate act of the nation, and with such a spirit of justice and humanity, as ought to silence all scruples about the validity of what has been done." If a revolution, such as the French, ran counter to these standards, then the United States was absolved of any commitment to that nation. In a later note to Secretary of State Thomas Jefferson, Hamilton contended that " a general invitation to revolution and insurrection, under a promise of fraternity and assistance . . . is not justifiable. Such a step is of a nature to disturb the repose of mankind, to excite fermentation in every country . . . and to endanger government everywhere."[21]

Among themselves, the older Federalists nervously mocked the analogy between the two revolutions. On his return from England in 1795, Jay toyed with the reverse of the analogy, proposing that, because the American Revolution had been a conservative event, any American who believed in the similarity of the two uprisings could expect that the French Revolution should be equally conservative: "If the intelligence is true that the French are forming a [new] Constitution and government similar to ours, that government will naturally discountenance such schemes and politics as may be hostile to it, and consequently will become cautious how they promote attacks on ours." Jay's correspondent, Secretary of War Timothy Pickering, evidently appreciated this satirical reversal of Francophilic arguments, for he repeated its substance to Charles Cotesworth Pinckney shortly before Pinckney departed to explain Jay's treaty to the French. "Your own observations," the secretary also told the minister plenipotentiary, "will furnish abundant proofs of the zeal . . . with which the people of the United States embraced the cause of the French revolution." Indeed, Pickering continued, the zeal was so great that it spilled out onto the streets in mobs and infiltrated to the very core of government. Tangled in Talleyrand's machinations during the XYZ controversy, John Marshall put the consensus of the "party of order" simply: "It is in America and America only that human liberty has found an Asylum. . . . [France] is not and never will be a republick." Marshall, Jay, Pickering, and Pinckney agreed that American Francophiles were men of passion, with a love for outlandish and inflamed historical comparisons, whereas anti-French men of affairs contented themselves with sober thoughts.[22]

For other Federalists drawn from the youths of 1776, the analogy between the two revolutions was too frightening to ridicule. Writing to Rufus King, Ames gasped at the consequences of the Francophilic parallel: "Jacobinism now uses and urges democracy, as it did in France—we are now in the Roland and Condorcet act of our comedy—whether we go on to the Danton and Robespierre acts depends on time and accident." Jacobinism was frightening not because it was new or rowdy but because its very nature—its worship of novelty and demagogy—disrupted order and ignored authority. Once in the saddle, the Jacobins would overthrow settled government and established law.[23]

Among the voices raised in the "party of order" were those of New England clergymen among the young revolutionaries of 1776. From the early pages of the first chapter, this book has primarily concerned itself with secular thought and secular figures. Puritan history in America had always insisted upon an apartness to New England experience, for the Puritans saw themselves as God's pilgrims in the New World. The sermons of both young and old ministers conventionally assumed the separateness and superiority of American history long before the generation of 1776 walked upon the earth. As the first two chapters attempted to show, shifts in the young revolutionaries' ideas of history signified their modification of a Whig science of history, rather than an adoption of Puritan historiography. There were certainly budding clerics among these youths, however, and they passed through the first stages of adulthood with other revolutionaries. When they reached their middle age, in the 1790s, they also faced the challenge of generativity—of passing on to a new generation their faith and experience. They tended to be conservative in habits, dress, and political preferences, and, as with other Federalists, these learned clergy were troubled by the demands of French radicals. The historical writing of these clergymen indicates that they wrestled with uncertainty in trying to transmit their experience and ideas. For some, like Timothy Dwight, the fear that they would not be able to inculcate their values in a new nation showed itself (among other manifestations) as a progressive hardening of historical judgment. Dwight's historical ideas appeared in poetic form, at first as gentle (for he was a moderate theologian in the 1780s and early 1790s) praise for Connecticut. By 1795 his fears had soured his view of history. When he assumed the presidency of Yale, he donned the mantle of historical orthodoxy: history could be taught in only one way to ensure that its lesson of conservatism and obedience never be misunderstood.[24]

Jedidiah Morse, another Yale-trained divine, though more moderate than Dwight through the early 1790s, reached the same conclusion by mid-decade. The first editions of his *American Geography*, in the middle 1780s, were optimistically nationalistic. By 1794, he had seen an error in his ways. Morse viewed the appearance of the Jacobin clubs as proof that the "French party intended to uproot all of America's past and establish a French dictatorship on American soil." In 1794, Morse published an anguished historical appeal for "order and harmony" in his *American Universal Geography*. The Federalist government, which Morse described as the foremost bulwark of social order, "the most perfect, the best administered government" in the world, was "steadily opposed in all its important measures" by radical demagogues. Morse presented an account of law and religion in the various states' histories in his *American Geography*, hoping his readers would adopt his models for good government and sound religion. He concluded that only an educated and conservative clergy, protected by strong government, could preserve society in the future, as it had in the past. "Faction and party spirit," "wretchedness and meanness," and "chaos" disturbed every state except Connecticut, where an entrenched clergy (composed of men with views similar to Morse's), "who are numerous, able and harmonious and very respectable as a body, have hitherto preserved a kind of aristocratic balance in the very democratic government of the state. This happily operated upon the overbearing spirit of democracy." Morse's fervor bespoke the enmity of many in the revolutionary generation of established New England clergymen for French revolutionary irreligion. On other occasions, Morse pleaded for the reawakening of "Christian religion and its sacred institutions, spurned at and rejected" in France and, he feared, in America after the French Revolution. It did not escape these clerics that Jefferson and others in his party were not so conventionally churchgoing as they might have been. Whether the Republicans were irreligious themselves, or merely the pawns of French impiety and philosophical anticlericalism, did not matter, for without the rituals and customs of religion, its doctrines would lose their power to move the spirit of the young.[25]

Out of their own chronicles of the republic and their criticism of the Jeffersonian version of history, the mature Federalists fashioned a general theory of American history that supplied their need to preserve the past. The mature Federalists were convinced that national survival depended upon already established American institutions. This was an exploration of the portion of revolutionary historical thought dismissed by the Jeffersonians among the generation of 1776. The "party of order" prayed that the dangers of French-inspired radicalism, cynicism, and democracy could be exposed as well as countered by exhibition of the personal virtue and conservatism of past generations of Americans. In the same way that such Francophiles as Madison and Jefferson used American revolutionary precedent as evidence for their case that the American Revolution would remain incomplete if the French republic failed, so the enemies of the French Revolution found that America's historic principles were antagonistic to French disorderliness, and republicanism at home was endangered by the agitation of the French interest.

The historical formula of the aging Federalists for the survival of the republic began with xenophobia. It proved a short step from condemnation of the French influence to the broader thesis that foreign influences always threatened America's native liberties. This was true, Francophobes reasoned, because America's treasured institutions evolved from purely native stock, and her liberty could be discovered in the first settlers' town meetings and burgesses. Unlike the French, who had erased their history, Americans had preserved their past in living political, social, and religious institutions. Americans were a different people—a people who had known how to create and preserve liberty in orderly fashion. In 1790, one year after John Adams had returned from England to assume the office of vice-president, he explained his distrust of the French experiment in terms of the generativity of conservatism:

Americans! Rejoice, that from experience you have learned wisdom and instead of whimsical and fantastical projects you have adopted a promising essay towards a well-ordered government. Instead of following any foreign example, to return to the legislation of confusion, contemplate the means of restoring decency, honesty, and order in society, by *preserving and completing*, if anything should be found necessary to complete the balance of your government. In a well-balanced government, reason, conscience, truth, and virtue, must be respected by all parties and exerted for the public good. [My italics.]

The French were trying to ignore their own history—a tale of oppression and demoralization—but they would not succeed. The past was never dead chronicle; it was habit and custom, values and ways of seeing, that lived in the present and must be transmitted to the next generation if the American republic were to survive.[26]

Mature Federalists insisted that the republic would be safe only when the habits and ideas that had gone into its creation were protected. Noah Webster, driven into a far deeper conservatism as the decade passed, surrounded by other Federalists' anxiety at the progress of French radicalism, expressed this tenet of historical conservatism in a letter to Jefferson. Webster dramatically denied any sympathy for history-as-process. Instead, he embraced the theory of the "corporate structure" of the state and built upon it a conception of a fixed, orderly, stable national history. Jefferson's creed that a people should not be bound by the will of past generations was particularly objectionable to the Connecticut educator: "that the members of a corporation [the State] cannot express the will of that corporation without a meeting for the purpose, and as this is impossible, no instructions of individual members can be binding . . . that every right claimed by a citizen of the government is liable to vary with circumstances, except what rest wholly on the moral law; that therefore every right created by political law should be always subject to be modified by the power that created it, viz, the will of the State." Only when the will of the people was embodied in their established institutions could popular consent be equated with true national law. The wisdom, order, and authority of the past ought not be dismissed by the whims of a new generation. Webster had come to believe the key to the health of republicanism lay in teaching young people to revere the past. The best defense against evil novelties, he wrote in 1796, was to place historical instruction in the hands of those "who feel a partiality for their native country, their laws, government and prosperity."[27]

As Webster's xenophobic thesis implied that America's liberties were not only unique but also the product of a long, evolutionary process, so his assertion of the conservatism of earlier generations of Americans implied that Americans had traditionally valued law, order, and "free debate and mature deliberation." This conclusion fit the Francophobes' abhorrence of radical and violent change. In Humphreys's words, the ideal was "choice free and frequent, yet no lust of change." Dwight discovered that, unlike Europeans, "Americans adored peace and tranquility." He captured this culminating historical thesis of the Francophobes—that American history was a saga of obedience to law and authority—in his pastorale, *Greenfield Hill*. Dwight first proposed that Americans had never before been influenced by speculative radical philosophy:

> Philosophy
> Would bow to common sense; and Man, from facts,
> And real life, political wisdom learn.

Americans always shunned European influences in favor of order:

> Ah then, thou favored land, thy self revere!
> Look not to Europe . . . of silly pomp, and manners
> trained to adore
> . . . of greybeard systems and meteoric dreams
> . . . of devastation; earth wet-deep with blood

. . . say then, ah say, woulds't thou for these exchange
The sacred institutions? thy mild laws?
Thy pure religion, morals, uncorrupt?
Order, peace, and general weal?

Reliance upon native virtues taught conservatism and stirred
Americans' love of order. Dwight's final injunction, like John
Adams's and Noah Webster's, was

Cherish still, watch, hold,
And hold through every trial
. . . all that is thine.[28]

As incisively as Jefferson's "the earth belongs in usufruct to
the living" encapsulated a theory of regeneration based upon
reform, so Dwight's poem captured the Federalist view of
regeneration through conservation. If Jefferson's view of history possessed the power to change men and institutions,
violently if necessary, to avoid corruption, so Dwight's history
stood as an impregnable fortress in the face of new and foreign dangers. To him and his fellow Federalists of the generation of 1776, the secret of parental responsibility for the
republic lay in the stability and virtue of individuals, but-
tressed by tested and proven instruments of government. Orderly men preserving an orderly society were the only hope
of national safety. To alter government and law violently was
to alter American historical development unnaturally and
thereby undermine the power of good men to direct events.
Shortly before he died, Hamilton summarized this thesis in
words that epitomize his own generative efforts as well as the
credo of his party: "The safety of a republic depends essentially on the energy of a common national sentiment; on a
uniformity of principles and habits; on the exemption of the
citizens from foreign bias, and prejudice; and on that love of
country which will almost invariably be found to be closely
connected with birth, education and family."[29]

To Hamilton and others, George Washington became the symbol of the connection between conservatism and generativity; his life and values were a model for generations to come. He was a living father for the country, a paragon of parental concern. His manner embodied continuity, authority, and sobriety, replacing the deposed father-king (and, in a sense, became the rallying point for the Federalists that the French Revolution was for early Republicans). Such fathers are often compelling examples for children when the latter grow into the heads of their own families—in this case the younger revolutionaries now in the Federalist party. After witnessing Washington's first inaugural, Ames had written: "It was a very touching scene, and quite of the solemn kind. . . . It seemed to me an allegory in which virtue was personified, and addressing those whom she would make her votaries. Her power over the heart was never greater, and the illustration of her doctrine by her own example was never more perfect." Washington was the father they had sought in 1776, and, more important to them as mature revolutionaries in the 1790s, he was a model for mature leadership: an example not just of policy, but of the way to transmit the values behind policy to a new generation. To Ames and others, he was history teaching by example—order and self-discipline personified.[30]

Beneath the historical broadsides in this combat over national policy lay the striving of mature family men to carry on the procreative tasks of fathers of the republic. Under these promptings, mature individuals will sift and review their past for its most important lessons, but for the generation of 1776, the "past" had a broader context. When Hamilton argued that the future of the republic rested upon "birth, education, and family" he was not speaking of his own childhood but of the collective birth, education, and domestication of the new nation. For the revolutionary generation, the past was nothing less than the history of the Revolution. This may seem a grandiose and arrogant presumption to a modern reader, but the revolutionaries, long upon the public stage and convinced of their just claims to fame, naturally shifted their thoughts back and forth between personal experiences and the great events of the three decades of nation-building. Thus Hamilton, in the midst of the struggle to ensure the supremacy of the Federalist party, and with it all of his own axioms of republican stewardship, cried out to Washington that the French party "are ready to *new model* our constitution, under the *influence* or *coercion* of France." One must remember that the writing and later interpretation of the Constitution, through the agency of the Federalist party, was the work of his lifetime and that Hamilton genuinely feared the radicalism of the Francophiles. He could not tolerate the thought that the work of his hands and heart might be misused by others. He dreaded that the legacy that he, as a Founding Father, wished to present to a new generation, was about to be destroyed.[31]

On the other side of the political fence, Elbridge Gerry moaned: "It has been unfortunate for their country, that the new [federal] constitution has divided the people, and enabled those who were disaffected to the revolution and who only supported the constitution as a stepping stone to monarchy, to avail themselves of the denomination of a party and styl[e] themselves federalists." In truth, the Federalists whom Gerry accused were not antagonistic to the Revolution—no more so than Jefferson or Gerry intended to deliver the federal government into the hands of French Jacobins—but Gerry's emotion had roots in the same tender, tutorial urge as Hamilton's. From the moment Gerry walked out of the Philadelphia Constitutional Convention in protest, he had viewed himself as an advocate of true revolutionary republicanism against monarchical consolidation of national power. Hamilton's indefatigable efforts to strengthen the national government and make war upon French radicalism had driven Gerry to question Hamilton's commitment to republicanism. Gerry concluded that such a man could not be trusted to inculcate revolutionary sentiments in a new generation.[32]

With history as their guide, the "party of liberty" and the "party of order" posed solutions to the challenge of regeneration that were creative and appropriate for the new republic. In the 1780s, these men had proclaimed that fundamental laws in the new nation, unlike any that had preceded it, were designed to promote the fullest expression of individual liberty, while providing for the due authority of government. Whether in power or in opposition during the 1790s, the mature revolutionaries found ways to give substance to their earlier boast. They found the materials to build a viable political structure upon the constitutional framework of the 1780s. The mature individual needs order—a sense of progression and achievement, a foundation for self-worth. The mature individual also needs liberty—the right and power to decide things for himself, to be himself, to continue to grow and change. In the public arena, the clash over generative ideology ended with a creative mixture of the two ideals of liberty and order: a democratic constitutionalism. Its crowning achievement was the two-party system, a stable, effective vehicle for the transmission of political ideals and policies from one generation to the next. Parental motives were served, for the personal quest of the mature revolutionaries to hand down their great experiment to the next generation flourished in public institutions surrounding the political parties: democratic electoral canvasses, rotation in office, and open political dissent.

But the psychic toll of the clash of histories was immense. In 1794, David Ramsay, a Federalist and a Francophile managing somehow to stand above the virulence of party, gave voice to the sincere goal of both parties: "France is daily proving, that a handful of citizens, fighting under the banners of liberty, is more than a match for an host of mercenaries, engaged in support of tyranny. It remains for us to recommend free governments, by the example of a peaceable, orderly, virtuous and happy people." Ramsay hoped in vain for reconciliation among the aging revolutionaries. The 1790s left them scarred and wary. Although the hardening of lines in the debates of the 1790s truly hurt them, they had pressed on because their generative motive was so basic to human needs. Small disputes grew into larger ones, cliques became factions, and factions organized themselves into parties because public debates of historical differences expressed fundamental personal needs. Angered or uneasy at the words of critics, tired of rethinking and reweighing their past, party leaders came to hear and consult only their allies. Extreme positions within both camps gradually became rival orthodoxies under the dual demands of internal needs and external criticism. Men once deeply attached to each other, co-workers in a great enterprise, began to hate each other. And the fury of partisanship, the abusive meetings and harsh letters, would never be wholly forgotten.[33]

Worst of all, the polarization of revolutionary historical ideas meant that the Founding Fathers had to defend one part of their experience against another part. All had loved liberty; all had sacrificed some portion of that liberty for social and political order. The historical debates of the 1790s forced each of them to make war upon a part of themselves, to separate ideas that had hitherto been fruitfully integrated in their minds. That they could do this to their own beliefs in the name of the regeneration of the republic, and still direct their efforts into effective political and intellectual channels, is testimony to the degree to which the needs of the eighteenth-century self could be sublimated to the higher good of public life. The inevitable by-product of this compartmentalization of historical ideas was to distance the public conduct of the once-young revolutionaries of 1776 from their inner lives, to make them ill at ease with the picture they themselves painted of political reality. Accusations and arguments were exaggerated, and friendships, like Adams's and Jefferson's, or Edmund Randolph's and Washington's, which had survived many crises, broke upon these shoals. The now-aging revolutionaries would have to deal with this artificial, self-deceiving separation of inner and outer lives when public tasks no longer occupied their attention.

CHAPTER FOUR

The Renunciation of History: Ego Integrity, 1800–1840

R etirement from politics saw the Founding Fathers re-
lieved of power and reduced in influence but no less
concerned for the fate of their great common endeavor.
Once caretakers of the republic and able to submerge personal anxiety in public feats, they now had the time to take
stock of themselves. They approached death, and with it the
prospect of fame or ignominy. Death may be the great leveler
of commoners and kings, but the old revolutionaries still had
something to fear from their passing beyond the loss of life.
Their ideas and reputations, so long in their own hands, would
pass to others. How would the future treat them? The prospects seemed favorable, for the previous generation of revolutionary heroes—led by Washington and Franklin—was laid
to rest with extravagant praise and almost no mention of partisanship or personal foibles. Even Hamilton, one of the cen-
ters of controversy among young men of the Revolution, was
eulogized with bipartisan good feeling. Like Hamilton, all of
the young men of 1776 held prominent offices and published
their views. They had played their parts in the founding of
the nation and could expect fame as their reward. But fame
came only with death, and death meant the loss of control of

their private treasures of ideas and feelings. For the aging revolutionary generation, retirement was thus a time of sincere and sometimes desperate musing on the meaning of their lives.[1]

Integrity was a word that the now old Founding Fathers caressed. For the sake of his integrity, John Adams opened his heart and memory to Hezekiah Niles's newspaper. Wasting from his wounds at Aaron Burr's hands, Hamilton insisted he had acted properly in the quarrel. Six years before his death, Jefferson's integrity drove him to reexamine the dark corners of his career. Old age is a time of stock-taking, during which one's integrity may be prized or cuffed. The revolutionary generation did not have modern therapies to aid them in self-evaluation, but they did have a treasured friend. In old age, they completed the merger of their own history with the history of the republic they had made and rummaged through the second for keys to the value of the first. The effort was painful and uncertain, but the strongest of them emerged from it with serenity of judgment. To appreciate this effort we must unravel the last of the puzzles in their idea of history.

In their youth, the young men of the Revolution had fused public concerns and personal needs into a new identity for themselves and their country. In maturity, they were the builders and managers of republicanism. The history that they wrote, the history that they created, was a constant reminder of these feats. Yet—and here is a last paradox in their historical thought—in old age the revolutionaries apparently dismissed the historical discipline and denigrated its utility. Did they? This paradox is most puzzling, for it marked the apparent renunciation of one medium by which this generation had defined itself. In the crisis of the 1760s, their invention of a separate American history had comforted and guided them through a bewildering world of conflicting loyalties. Their novel historical ideas told them who they were and what they must do to be men. In the years of war and constitution-making that followed, the exclusivistic national history they fashioned pointed the way toward true intimacy with their fellow revolutionaries. Even when, under the pressures of diplomatic and domestic partisanship, differing views of the "true" history of the Revolution led them down vituperative paths, these paths eventually ended in a resolution of the challenge of generativity. In truth, history had been their *magister vitae*.

There was nothing novel in complaints about particular historical versions of the past. History was a tool of politics, invariably bound up in partisanship. The young men of 1776 lived in an age of revealed and reviled ambition in whose chronicling almost all of the revolutionary generation had joined at one time or another. Failing powers did not blur the memory or balm the sting of previous historical confrontations. If the revolutionaries' animadversions on party history stopped where the debates of the 1790s stopped—with criticism of an opponent's historical views—there would be no paradox to examine. After 1800, in a note here and there, building steadily to a crescendo, one can hear a new refrain—renunciation of the *discipline itself*. It was not this history or that history which merited abuse, but all histories, for intrinsic failings. This was a vast sea change in their thinking, at odds with their previous view of history. Their renunication of history could not be laid at the door of partisanship, for not only was the criticism nonpartisan, it struck at the very heart of partisan history by denying that history had any relevance at all for politics.

The progress of their disillusionment was not linear. Their dismay with history waxed and waned and varied from individual to individual. But all arrived at the same disgust with history, and all considered renunciation of it. Their anger was clear in the 1800s, though it was obscured by and sometimes merged into the furious polemical wars of that decade. When

political passions cooled after the War of 1812, the old revolutionaries persisted in their attack upon history. Though
younger politicians found comfort in patriotic history, their
mentors made war upon the past—their past—with bitter
words.

In the furious political wars of the 1800s, we encounter
fragments of this new, ominously disgruntled view of history—that history is, after all is said and done, quite useless
to men of affairs. After he left office, John Adams declared
that prejudice and partisanship were usurping the place of
reason in the writing of history and lamented "I doubt whether
impartial history ever was or can be written." Forced into
retirement by the Republicans and abused by his own party,
Adams told Federalist William Cunningham, "I wish to remain in obscurity, and by no means to become the subject of
conversation or speculation." In 1802, John Marshall, Adams's
appointee as chief justice, assumed that the "political tem-
pests which will long, very long, exist" would spawn partisan
historians, and later burned many of his personal papers in
disgust. Philadelphia democrat Benjamin Rush disconso-
lately wrote Adams in 1805, "Perceiving how widely [his
memoir of the Revolution] should differ from the historians
of that event, and how much I should offend by telling the
truth, I threw my documents into the fire."[2]

Perhaps in the 1800s, mingled with still-glowing embers of
party grievances there was now a jealousy of the younger
generation of scholars and politicians who were inheriting
the works for which the older revolutionaries had bled. As
guardians of the true histories of the Revolution, the repositories of which were their own memories, it was natural for
the surviving Founding Fathers to lament the injustices of
younger historians. Adams particularly feared that the Revolution itself might not be satisfactorily studied by the next
generation. "Can you account," he wrote to Thomas McKean,
"for the apathy, the antipathy, of this nation to their own

history?" Jefferson shared Adams's unease that declining interest in American history would undermine the experiment begun by the revolutionary leaders. "What is to become of our past revolutionary history?" he repeatedly quizzed his old comrades. In these pleas there is impatience and even desperation that the next generation would betray the hopes and sacrifices of the revolutionaries by believing the fabrications of partisan scribblers.[3]

The old revolutionaries' disillusionment with history went farther than exasperation with partisanship and feelings of misuse by their juniors, though the latter may have occasioned some public expressions of their new sentiments. One reads a deeper regret in the words of the first of the aging revolutionaries to approach renunciation: Hamilton, Ames, and Rush. Early in the 1800s, they decried both personal and public dangers in the misuse of history. They feared that the meaning of their actions and the motives for their words would never, indeed, could never, be recovered when they were gone from the scene. Their motive was not that they saw their own demise approaching (though in fact all were to die soon after they penned these thoughts on history), but a raging despair with the present.

Hamilton's disgust exploded in an October 1800 *Letter . . . Concerning the Public Conduct and Character of John Adams.* This pamphlet, written against the advice of Hamilton's friends within the Federalist party, was a catastrophe for its author as well as for Federalist election hopes in 1800. From the moment of its publication, he lost command of his party and all hopes for higher office. Hamilton persisted in writing it, and when parts of it leaked out in the Republican party press he willingly published the whole. The *Letter* was not primarily about Adams but about the historical reputation of Hamilton. Adams had done much to undermine Hamilton's foreign policy and military standing during the latter part of 1799. Hamilton replied with the *Letter*, to "repel these slanders; by stating the real views of the persons who are calumniated and the reasons of their conduct." To repair his reputation, Hamilton turned to history, from "an earlier period" of the American Revolution to the crisis of 1799. The *Letter* is written almost entirely in the first person. It records Hamilton's first impressions of Adams and justifies Hamilton's later conduct as secretary of the treasury, adviser to Washington, and confidant of Adams's cabinet. Hamilton's decision to "resist" the influence of foreign powers supposedly led to "the persecution I have endured in the subsequent stages of my political life," but he did not wish to be remembered as a monarchist or a tool of Britain. Adams was a real political opponent—no doubt of that exists—but Hamilton did not write to smear or destroy Adams. Hamilton even concluded the *Letter* with praise for Adams as a person and gave half-hearted support for Adams's candidacy (though Hamilton stated that Charles C. Pinckney was to be preferred). There was a quiet desperation in the *Letter*, a supplicating tone that swept Hamilton beyond the bounds of political decorum and practicality. His closest political allies realized this, though they incorrectly credited it to Hamilton's dislike of Adams. He had laid himself bare, begging to be understood by those who might think him a man greedy for power and rank. Hamilton would later regain his composure and re-enter the pamphleteering lists, but the anxiety he felt for the judgment of history against his views during his forced retreat from power was an omen of the renunciation of history soon embraced by other surviving revolutionaries. He would lament, shortly before he died: "In vain was the collected wisdom of America convened at Philadelphia. In vain were the anxious labors of a Washington bestowed."[4]

In the last days of Federalist rule and the first years of Republican tenure, Fisher Ames's despair exceeded Hamilton's. The Massachusetts Federalist prophesied the imminent fall of the new nation. The decline of Federalism and his own political fortunes profoundly discouraged him. He warned that the election of Jefferson was no mere alternation of parties. He was a "fool," he admitted, for placing his faith in historical essays and instruction, for they had no effect on the course of history. "Why should I consume my marrow with the fires of that zeal that seems ridiculous to my friends." The source of his distrust lay not in the triumph of a few "Jacobins" or in their party's popularity but in the "political theories of our country and in ourselves." He had finally discovered that American history itself was the enemy, for its lessons were insufficient for its citizens' instruction: "There is a kind of fatality in the affairs of republics, that eludes the foresight of the wise as much as it frustrates the toils and sacrifices of the patriot and the hero." Instead of mastering history, and through its lessons controlling change, "we have all the time floated, with a fearless and unregarded course, down the stream of events." Helpless to fend off the Jeffersonian assault within the public arena, powerless to console himself with the effort of writing essays, he turned on the once boastful, supposedly powerful tutor of those words—American history—and dismissed it.[5]

Hamilton's self-criticism and Ames's self-pity may easily be attributed to the sad fate of Federalism. They despaired of history—perhaps—because it had taken a wrong turn. Both men were angry and bewildered at their party's fall. But the source of Hamilton's and Ames's lament lies deeper than electoral politics. Old Republicans, who should have gloried in their party's rise, also turned on history. Benjamin Rush's anguish with history rivaled that of Ames. Mistreated by his enemies in the 1790s, he pronounced himself "a stranger in my native state," a man without a history. Unwilling to admit to his own partisan instincts, he defended himself against others' partisanship not only by retiring from politics but by denying both his own role in the revolutionary history of Pennsylvania and the more general utility of history in polit-

ical life. "Permit me to congratulate you upon your recovering
your freedom and independence by retiring to private life,"
he wrote former Secretary of War James McHenry, recalling
his own divorce from public service. "Public measures and
public men appear very differently to persons who see them
at a distance from what they appear to persons who are actors
in or under them." Never hesitating to speak his mind, even
to a man from the other party, Rush warned McHenry that
history written by its own protagonists could never be fair to
individuals and that politicians could never expect justice from
the essays of their opponents. He knew that the history he
rejected was the experience of his own generation. In attack-
ing history he therefore questioned the accomplishments of
the revolutionaries. In Jefferson, also bruised by scurrilous
partisanship, he hoped to find a kindred spirit. On March 15,
1813, he asked the retired Republican president: "From the
present complexion of affairs in our country, are you not dis-
posed at times to repent of your solicitude and labors and
sacrifices during our Revolutionary struggle for liberty and
independence?" As damaging as it may have been for individual revolutionaries to rest their reputations and hopes for
the future in historical labors, it was even more dangerous
for them to believe that they, or others, could learn from
histories. In his "Travels" (1800) he recalled his youthful discovery about the Continental Congress: "I now [in 1774] saw
that men do not become wise by the experience of other people
. . . with the best dispositions to act properly, the people of
America imitated the blunders of nations in situations similar
to their own, and scarcely succeeded in a single undertaking
till they had exhausted all the errors that had been practiced
in the same pursuits in other countries." Later reflection in-
formed him that his people did not even learn from their own
experience: "But what avail reading, reflection, experience
and American birth in the present state of our country?" Rush
told a sympathetic John Adams in 1812, "It would seem as if

we had read history not to avoid but to imitate the blunders of those who had gone before us." This was the use Americans had actually made of history; only pride in their own accomplishments, which is to say in themselves, had led them to expect more from the discipline.[6]

Although the animosities and partisanships that beseiged Hamilton, Ames, and Rush in the 1800s and climaxed in the War of 1812 were cooled by the peace of Ghent, older revolutionaries did not cease complaining about history. Instead, the survivors of the revolutionary generation expanded upon their doubts and fears for history even as their younger political successors embraced the patriotic, nonpartisan style of historical declamation popular after the war. The years after the War of 1812 brought forth an abundance of annals of historical societies and patriotic historical displays (occasionally soliciting the attendance of the aged survivors of 1776). The old revolutionaries' growing dismay with history was not matched among younger politicians after 1815. John Quincy Adams, Henry Clay, and Daniel Webster, to name a few of the next generation's leaders, were all adept and confident in their interpretations of historical lessons. The old revolutionaries swam against the tide in their condemnation of historical lessons. If the dramatic realignment of parties after 1815 had any effect upon the historical notions of the last of the revolutionaries, it was to deepen their sense of foreboding and alienation from their own past.[7]

Gouverneur Morris of New York had lost patience with "presumptuous writers, affecting knowledge they do not possess, [who] undertake to instruct mankind by specious stories, founded on idle rumour and vague conjecture . . . such writings, tho' sheltered by contempt, from contemporaneous contradictions, are raked out, in a succeeding age, from the ashes of oblivion, and relied on as authority. History, compiled from such materials, can hardly teach us the science of human nature." At his place of retirement on the Hudson,

Jay read Morris's talk, and communicated his agreement to his old comrade: "Your strictures on the defects of history, and the causes of them, are well founded. Whether future historians, with all their advantages, will excel their predecessors in accuracy, and caution, and candor, is a point on which my expectations are not sanguine." This was the same Jay who once assured McDougall that posterity always did justice and who later encouraged Jedidiah Morse, a fierce party man, to prepare a new history of the Revolution. By 1816, Jay's opinion of history had indeed altered. His comment to Morris was sincere, and he told Judge Richard Peters, "An accurate and well written history of the United States down to the conclusion of the late war [of 1812] is desirable, but my expectations on that head are not sanguine."[8]

So disgusted, after 1815, was Marshall with the historical wars of the 1790s and 1800s that he sought refuge in semianonymity. His biography of Washington had presented the case for the party of order at great length, but the work was poorly reviewed in some quarters, and Marshall spent his last years revising, correcting, and apologizing for it. For a genial, often sloppy man continually to beg forgiveness for spelling errors suggests that something far deeper in the reception of the volumes disturbed him. He had unsuccessfully tried to keep his name off the title page and, in a larger way, to keep himself out of politics. A chief justice of his political stature could hardly accomplish this feat. He did not always follow his own directive, particularly in his private correspondence, but with each renewal of party struggle, each contest of local against national government, he became more anxious that he might be considered a partisan and so contribute, however inadvertently, to the weakening of national institutions. After 1815, he refused to appear at events commemorating any partisan victory and eventually came to deny the reality of his own part in history as surely as did Rush. Old differences of opinion gave him increasing pain, and though his capacity for dispute was not dulled, his willingness to enter disputes faded.

When Adams's letters to William Cunningham were published by Cunningham's Republican son, revealing Adams's intemperate anger at other Federalists, Marshall lamented: "I feel great respect for Mr. Adams, and shall always feel it whatever he may do. The extreme bitterness with which he speaks of honorable men who were once his friends is calculated to mortify and pain those who remain attached to him." Marshall himself had labored to avoid mention of similar episodes. About Jefferson, his arch political enemy, he insisted, "I have never allowed myself to be excited (or intimidated) by Mr. Jefferson's unprovable and unjustifiable aspersions on my conduct and principles." Marshall's anger could not be concealed, but his self-censorship—his denial of what really transpired between the two men, with all its importance for the course of history—indicated his effort to insulate himself from the past. To Timothy Pickering, whose extreme Federalism Marshall had eschewed, and whose attacks on Adams Marshall must have found objectionable, the chief justice returned bland praise: "Your recollection of events which took place for the last twenty years is very accurate and you replace in my memory many things which I had almost forgotten." Marshall did not add that he was trying to forget those events. What he did say had the same implication: "There are not many who retain these events as fresh as you do, and I am persuaded that they will soon be entirely lost. Those who follow us will know very little of the real transactions of our day, and will have very untrue impressions respecting men and things."[9]

If, as Marshall found, history could not be totally escaped, it might perhaps be drained of the venom of regret and loss. With disillusionment and pain in his recollection of former ideals, Rufus King complained to Christopher Gore in 1816, "We have been the visionary men, who have believed, as many have, that mere paper constitutions, without those moral and political habits and opinions, which alone give solidity and support to any government, would be sufficient to protect and preserve the equal rights of the weak against the strong." As the threat of mental anguish lay in the memory of past ideals, so the cure might lie in the destruction of history. If the past was irrelevant to the present, then history could be safely ignored, if not made to disappear. A short time after his lament to Gore, King wrote, "I have considered our party struggle as at an end, and am not inclined anywhere, on any occasion, in the discussion of measures concerning the general welfare, to introduce our party divisions . . . I am perfectly willing to leave to future times the decision of which party was faithful and intelligent, and which best consulted the true interests of the country. No present discussion can affect this decision." King felt the cruel blows of postwar antifederalist feeling; any device to avert recollection of earlier pain must have been inviting.[10]

In the 1810s and 1820s, aged Republican survivors of the revolutionary generation expressed themselves as distraught as retired Federalists at the future utility of history. Jefferson felt control over the past slipping away as surely as his personal and political influence. "We have been too careless of our future reputation," he told a fellow Republican, "while our Tories will omit nothing to place us in the wrong." Marshall's *Life of Washington* galled him, and he confessed in his introduction to his "Anas" that "were a reader of this period to form his ideas of it from this history alone, he would suppose the Republican party . . . were a mere set of grumblers, and disorganizers, satisfied with no government." Chroniclers like Marshall and John Quincy Adams seemed partial, passionate, and venomous. Jefferson, always more fervent in private conversation than in public, could not forbear appending a critical review of Hamilton's career to his journal. This, written in 1818, was redolent of the partisan broadsides of twenty years before. Hamilton and his friends were "monarchists in principle" who labored to undermine the republic. But the aged Jefferson did not rush to publish his "Anas" as he had, in 1798, sought to promulgate his objections to the Alien and Sedition Acts. Nothing was to be gained by publication; there was no weapon against the misuse of history, no insurance that the truth would prevail over partisan lies. "History," he lamented, "may be made to wear any hue, with which the passions of the compiler, royalist or republican, may choose to tinge it." In 1818, Jefferson aimed not at building a new world order upon historical knowledge of the past but sought simple justice to the memory of Thomas Jefferson. He told Francis Gilmer of Virginia, "I have no pretensions. If the rancorous vituperations of enemies . . . can only be reduced by time to their just estimate, it will more than fill the measure of my humble prospects."[11]

The pervasive and passionate disgust of the revolutionary remnant with history after the war of 1812 should be credited at its face value. Their indictment—like Hamilton's, Ames's and Rush's—was as sweeping as their faith had once been. They did not see a time or a nation that had or would produce just histories, and they warned others against relying upon the disinterested discretion of historical accounts, as they had once done. We should not, however, accept their own explanation for their disillusionment without further examination. They insisted that they rejected history because it, and not they themselves, had changed; history had become corrupted by partisanship. This argument cannot be conceded, for there was no more partisan and self-interested period of American historical thinking than the revolutionary years and no better historical special pleaders than the young revolutionaries. It is possible that, in the heat of their bitterness at the partisanship of the nineteenth century, they forgot their own role in the party wars, their sponsorship of historical polemic? Their ascription of their renunciation of history to its new partisanship is riddled with even more palpable inconsistencies. Their dislike of partisanship was genuine, but they had recognized, earlier in their lives, that historical writing was an expressive weapon, responsive to the needs and desires of its wielders. Their own commitment to historical reasoning, their need to explain and defend political positions with historical arguments, had dragged the discipline into partisan confrontations. External considerations also refute their reason for rejecting history: the younger politicians around the aged revolutionaries did not follow their elders' course, but continued to embrace history. The relevant question is not, then, what was the effect of partisanship upon the old revolutionaries' views of history, but when and why did partisanship become so fearful and threatening to them that it disrupted their sense of their own past and destroyed their mastery over the revolutionary experience.

In reality, history acted as a substitute for something far more threatening. The latter, the root cause of their anxiety, was aroused by the persistence of partisan history. One must first scrutinize the timing of their rejection of history. It came in the period in their lives, not the same biological age for all of them, but an equivalent stage in the life cycle, when they left office, or removed themselves from active public life, or began to feel irreversible physical and mental decline. At the same time, they noticed the passing of their comrades and felt the approach of their own demise. As young men, they had been confident of their use of history and its identification of their place in human events, because, as young men, they could look forward to long careers in public life. They could employ history to build a nation. In their maturity, this is what actually happened. As retired veterans of the political wars, they saw the history of the republic, the living tool forged by their lives and deeds, fall into other hands. The fact that they were not so well treated at these hands may have added to their anger and frustration at the betrayal of revolutionary history, but it was the loss of power and of control which they lamented.[12]

At the bottom of this phenomenon, one discovers that old age, or at least advanced age, retirement, and depleted capacities, was the leading cause of the revolutionaries' renunciation of historical study. In 1812, Jefferson was sixty-nine and Adams seventy-seven years old. The other revolutionaries were also advanced in years. To some extent, these were tired men, and historical debates only reminded them that the work of their generation was neither finished nor secure. As we have come to expect from this generation, personal dismay was inextricably bound up with fear for the public weal. Partisanship had brought private feelings and public positions into complex juxtaposition for men who labored with and against each other for so many years. In retirement or old age, the revolutionaries reversed this ordering of experience. They worried that repudiation of their own particular ideas or services in partisan histories was tantamount to the destruction of the republic. The appearance of partisan history aroused fear for the nation and thereby became intolerable to men who had done so much to build that nation and now could do no more for it. This explanation is convincing—but not complete. The revolutionaries, even in retirement, did not shun controversy. They proffered opinions on slavery, constitutional revision in the states, federal economic policy, and many other contemporary issues. They neither feared controversy nor rejected it—only histories of controversy and controversial histories.

The old age of the revolutionaries worked in a more profound way upon their views of history. The revolutionaries' assault on history was a questioning of their entire careers. Old age brings with it a final challenge, a last stage of maturation, according to Erikson:

116

Only in him who in some way has taken care of things and people and has adapted himself to the triumphs and disappointments adherent to being, the originator of others or the generator of products and ideas—only in him may gradually ripen the fruit of these . . . I know no better word for it than ego integrity. . . . It is a post-narcissistic love of the human ego—now of the self—as an experience which conveys some world order and spiritual sense, no matter how dearly paid for. It is the acceptance of one's one and only life cycle as something that had to be and that, by necessity, permitted of no substitutions. . . . It is a comradeship with the ordering ways of distant times and different pursuits, as expressed in the simple products and sayings of such times and pursuits. . . . For he knows that an individual life is the accidental coincidence of but one life cycle with but one segment of history; and that for him all human integrity stands or falls with the one style of integrity of which he partakes.

The revolutionary generation had grown older in the rhythms of a great historical epoch, yet for all their real achievements, they struggled with the nemesis of old age—despair: "The feeling that the time is now too short, too short for the attempt to start another life and to try out the alternative roads to integrity. Disgust hides despair, if often only in the form of 'a thousand little disgusts' which do not add up to one big remorse." By doubting the value of the discipline of history itself, they could indirectly question the value of their own past. They were the children of an age that kept private agonies separate and secret from popular view. These men were not given to the kind of public soul-searching that would have revealed their inner doubts to later generations. Jefferson had great "antipathy to the telling of anything about his public life," and Madison had no patience "with those who were curious about the details of personal or private life." Their questioning of history was the expression of the stock-taking of old age they permitted themselves.[13]

This is why, as they got older, they became more insistent upon a "correct" (meaning an emotionally fulfilling as well as intellectually satisfying) account of the Revolution. They demanded an external referent for their own understanding of what they achieved with their lives. Their rejection of history grew from a need to judge their lives and careers. They knew their days were coming to an end, and they wished history, their good and trustworthy mentor, to tell them if these days had been well spent. Was not history the record of public deeds, and were they not public men? History had always comforted and directed them. In old age, they asked history to prove the integrity, moral worth, and staying power of what they had done. They found instead scurrilous innuendo and mindless, partisan annals.

For such men as Marshall and King to deny the fact of partisanship was a denial not only of the reality of American history but of their own careers as well. Ames and Rush had traveled this road; Hamilton had set one foot upon it before his death. If this was the defense they chose against the anguish of reading history, their pain must have been great indeed. Their denials could be self-lacerating, as was John Adams's when he forecast to Jefferson, "Your character in history may easily be foreseen. Your administrations will be quoted by philosophers as a model of profound wisdom; by politicians as weak, superficial, and shortsighted. Mine, like a Pope's woman, will have no character at all." Or Jefferson's reply to a friendly correspondent: "You say I must go to writing history. While in public life, I had not the time, and now that I am retired, I am past the time. To write history requires a whole life of observation, of inquiry, of labor, and correction. Its materials are not to be found among the ruins of a decayed memory." A tired, ironic Jefferson implied that the employed public servant had no time for history, because history had little to do with the conduct of public life. How different this was from his views in the 1790s! In retirement, open to the blows of time and enemies, history availed one little. These are the laments of men who tremble that history has passed them by, and, in despair, strike out at it. They annihilated history, as it seemed poised to annihilate them.[14]

For some able and productive revolutionary leaders, this final challenge of the life cycle was too overwhelming to be faced squarely. To aging revolutionaries who refused to engage in a dialogue with their own past, history could become an embalming fluid, permanently preserving a lost world in a semblance of life. The dogged filiopietism of a few of this generation hid and soothed a gnawing despair with their own approaching demise, a more extreme defense against the passage of time than the denial of historical partisanship embraced by Rush, Marshall, and King. Filiopietism offered a more seductive, and ultimately unreal, refuge of fantasy: the belief or faith that the history of their portion of the world had not changed with time. Clinging to this fantasy of stasis, they struggled to escape the fate of mortals. David Humphreys and Noah Webster clung to the rock of New England history, not to save the region from foreign influences or democratic mobs (as Federalism had in the 1790s and 1800s) but to save themselves. By identifying himself with the timeless virtues of Connecticut, Humphreys gained a respite from mortality. Merged and identified with the strength of the state, his powers seemed unimpaired by the passage of years. He spoke thus for himself as well as for his home, when he wrote, "Connecticut, among the foremost in the struggle for independence, among the first to adopt the constitution, will not be the last to tamely suffer that independence to be lost, that constitution to be impaired." She, like Humphreys, would survive, "unchangeable." Through this mask of immutability, one can sense his isolation. David Hackett Fischer reminds us, "Because old age was very rare, the aged also suffered from a sense of isolation, loneliness and emptiness." Humphreys was not the first of his generation to feel keenly the loss of time and friends and to seek solace in the past.[15]

One could hardly say that Webster abandoned history in his prolonged old age, for, from 1800 to his death in 1840, he published a history of his country, a historical dictionary, and scores of letters of advice to young men stuffed with history. He continued to write and think about history—but, after the war, in a new framework. He became a rejuvenated Calvinist, a man redeemed by his surrender to faith and orthodoxy. Henceforth, he produced history in the service of religion and rejoiced that the divine hand of providence explained all things. This was a far cry from his mild antireligious sentiments during the Revolution and farther still from his advocacy of an enlightened and idealistic human history. History to the young revolutionary had been a purgative of superstition; to the old lexicographer, it was a proof of scripture. His *History of the United States*, published in 1835, began with Adam and Eve, traced the guiding power of religion in the Revolution, and pledged that America would always remain God's special land. Religious metahistory, without the pain of failure and criticism that had plagued him, brought sweetness, peace, and relief. To write it, the Lord "ha[d] sustained a feeble constitution, amidst obstacles and toils, disappointments, infirmities, and depression." Religion comforted him but did not curb his pessimism. Reconciliation with the recent past, that is, with his own part in history, also might have sustained him in old age as it had in the darkest hours of his youth, but history taught that high Federalism had failed, and this was an intolerable lesson. He had not abandoned history—but he had despaired so irrevocably of its quarrels, disorders, and disobedience—all symptomatic of democracy—that he emptied the history of his country of all its human content and refilled the shell with pious homily.[16]

The depth and yearning of Webster's conversion experience, as desperate as Humphreys's refusal to yield to old age,
hints at the dread which, in earlier years, command of history
held at bay. If, as Ernest Becker has written, the fear of death
"haunts the human animal like nothing else," driving sane
men, brilliant men, to denial, fabrication, and self-deluding
heroism, the crumbling of the past must have brought terror
to these aging Federalists. Timothy Pickering, rejected by a
new generation of Salem voters, spent his last days in long
walks and vigorous exercise. He literally refused to admit his
approaching fate; "it was his last great struggle." The Constitution and the first Federalist administrations were their
monument, their hedge against mortality. With Jeffersonian-
ism's steady gain in the popular mind, that monument was
no more. Character, integrity, and a willingness to face the
limitations of life—the irony of fame and death that were
described at the start of this chapter—would attune other
Federalists to their fate, but the "reality of life, the full problem of things," was brutal, when the refuges of a heroic past
were stripped away.[17]

Neither Humphreys, Webster, nor Timothy Dwight, the last
a patriarch of the Connecticut clergy by the time of his death
in 1817, could conceal their great sadness at the passing of a
world they had known in their prime of life. Humphreys
mourned: "The few surviving actors from the stage of the
revolutionary war will daily become more and more scarce."
His grief was mottled with anger at a younger generation that
did not respect their elders' achievements, and he raged pub-
licly, "We will leave this scene not for a tittering generation
who wish to push us from it." With old age Webster, too, had
grown increasingly insistent upon the frailty of human nature. Idealistic reforms were dangerous; safety lay in the tried
and tested. Dwight's posthumously published travel journals
insisted: "The observation of a single man will easily convince
him that the characteristical features of any body of men liv-

ing by themselves and particularly united in their concerns regularly descend through a long period to their posterity. The character of many towns and parishes in New England, where everything is progressive and changing, can now be traced with irresistible evidence to its first settlers. History in a more extensive and satisfactory manner evinces the same truth." On his deathbed Dwight despaired, for "since the American Revolution, our situation has become less favorable to the existence, as well as to the efficacy, of these great means of internal peace." A mature Dwight, in the midst of the party wars of the 1790s, had confidence in the generative power of New England history. Twenty years later, despite the "good feelings" of the postwar years, he succumbed to the self-abnegation of old age.[18]

The fantasy of an unchangeable past was not the only form of despair that preyed upon old age. Rage, displayed in vengeful historical mutterings, also bespoke rankling despondency. In Ames's and Rush's cases, this anger was self-directed. Pickering projected his despair at his own foreshortened career in angry historical attacks on others. Stung by publication of the Adams-Cunningham correspondence, Pickering assaulted the Braintree patriarch furiously. His *Review* of the letters was not history for truth's sake or for some discernible political end. It was born of frustration, over a career Adams sidetracked by sacking then Secretary of State Pickering many years before. Pickering admitted as much when he wrote, "What is history? A mere detail of events may engage curiosity; but it is the character of the actors which especially interest the reader." What followed was not a moral commentary of the Plutarchian sort but a collection of rumors and slurs. Jefferson suffered Pickering's rancor in the latter's preface to an 1823 reading of the Declaration of Independence in Salem. The occasion was hardly appropriate for Pickering's thrust. A partisan attack, especially one renewing contentions among the all-but-sanctified signers, must have surprised even stalwart Federalists in the audience. Pickering had been nipping at Jefferson's reputation for many years, and in 1823 he accused Jefferson outright of copying the language of the Declaration from common English sources and then claiming too much credit for himself. Ironically, Pickering used Adams's recollections as a source. Even the deaths of Jefferson and Adams three years later, occasions for the solemn celebration of their deeds among their countrymen, did not still Pickering's pen, for Pickering's canker gnawed within: history had abandoned him. Though he resolved on his death bed to record "truths, important in an historical point of view," he decided "it is of no matter," for " 'truths would you teach, or save a sinking land, All fear, none aid you, and few understand.' " [19]

None of the Founding Fathers was immune to such dejection. Jefferson showed flashes of passionate agony in his historical reminiscences. When he learned of the intrusion of slavery and sectionalism into the debate over Missouri's application for statehood, Jefferson lamented, "I regret that I am now to die in the belief, that the useless sacrifice of themselves by the generation of 1776, to acquire self-government and happiness to their country, is to be thrown away by the unwise and unworthy passions of their sons." James Madison, the recipient of many of Jefferson's historical complaints, promised to guard his older friend's historical reputation, but the shy, bookish master of Montpelier was also prey to moments of depression. Without Jefferson's passion, but with Jefferson's fears of disunion and slavery, Madison's words to his countrymen were often more resigned than hopeful: "The advice nearest to my heart and deepest in my convictions is that the Union of the states be cherished and perpetuated. Let the open enemy to it be regarded as a pandora with her box opened; and the disguised one, as the serpent, creeping with his deadly wiles into paradise." The making of the Constitution was to Madison's personal history (and as always with this generation, to the history of the republic) what the Declaration of Independence and the concept of personal liberty was to Jefferson's. When Madison despaired of the Union, as Jefferson did for liberty, it was fear of the negation of a life's work that spoke.[20]

Even as they abused history, that discipline served the revolutionary generation's innermost personal needs. Anger and disgust at oneself could be safely directed at history, and the self-destructiveness of despair could be thereby blunted. The renunciation of the discipline of history acted as a mechanism of defense against all the pain and doubt in their recollections. By lopping off a part of themselves—their role in the nation's history—they preserved the rest from the mortal admission of failure. The assault on history was an effective therapy for the strongest-minded of the revolutionaries, for it enabled them to criticize their own excesses while not calling into question their moral or intellectual values. History helped them, in the end, to accept their mortality and the safety of passing their great burden on to a new generation.[21]

Thus, although pessimism nagged at these men, and they occasionally bowed to it, as a whole they did not surrender. Angry with history, they did not resign themselves to its inutility, nor, therefore, to their own inconsequentiality in the saga of human events. Wearily shuttling between his home in Pittsburgh and his duties on the Supreme Court in Philadelphia, Brackenridge was the first of them to face and master the challenge of ego integrity. His wry but firm commitment to history guided his steps. Though he presided at court sessions sloppily dressed, often with his boots off and his feet resting on the bench, and his tall hunched figure seemed cloaked in gloom, he continued to write, and his essays and poems burned with the old fires. He was proud of his accomplishments and wished them preserved. He collected earlier *Pittsburgh Gazette* essays for publication in 1806, "not with a view to a long period of posthumous existence but that of a few years among my immediate descendants, who may take some little pride in preserving the memory of a literary man, and this for their own sakes." He had tried to bring law and learning, and a bit of the muse, to the frontier, and "though my fame must fall short of giving lustre to a country, yet it may throw a little light on a small circle of immediate descendants and endure, perhaps, for a generation after I am gone." He wished his contribution to survive in its literary form (he depreciated his political and judicial achievements), but he knew that form was not fictional. His most enduring literary works were barely disguised historical ones, and his magnum opus, *Modern Chivalry*, concluded with a plea for the value of the lessons he had learned in the past: "For this painting I claim credit; but I have more the useful in view than the amusing of the work. . . . 'All of which I saw and part of which I was.' I have myself been of the bar; have had to do, in a canvass for elections; and have been of a legislative body; like all young orators, I have babbled as others have done." Brackenridge dropped his persona, Captain Farrago, to address the reader directly in the closing passages of *Modern Chivalry*. Written in 1815, they pronounced a valedictory on his own small but worthy place in history.[22]

As his final days approached, Jefferson also brought himself to begin an autobiography: "At the age of 77," he wrote, "I begin to make some memoranda, and state some recollections of dates and facts concerning myself, for my own more ready reference, and for the information of my family." He set down soft words, not revising his judgment of history but signaling his own determination to face his past. To his friends, he signaled his dying affirmation of his role in history. He wrote Madison: "It has also been a great solace to me to believe that you are engaged in vindicating to posterity the course we have pursued . . . take care of me when [I am] dead." Shortly before he died, Jefferson replied to an invitation to celebrate the 1826 jubilee of independence. He was too infirm to go, but he seized the opportunity to stand in final judgment of the chief work of his life. Of the Declaration he wrote, "It will be (to some parts sooner, to others, later, but finally to all), the signal of arousing men to burst the chains under which monkish ignorance and superstition had persuaded them to bind themselves, and to assume the blessings and security of self-government. . . . All eyes were opened, or opening, to the rights of man." On the eve of his death Jefferson had come to terms with his past. In a fashion typical of his generation, he announced the resolution of his personal crisis of ego integrity to a political gathering.[23]

To the north, in Braintree, Adams triumphed over despair. He had worried and fussed in turn, lashing out against aristocracy, slavery, and pretension. Early in his retirement, his worst suspicions were expressed in asides on history. If the history of the Revolution was "now lost forever," then only the few who remained must tell the tale. He could not finish his autobiography—the pain of others' envy and insults was too great to bear. In letters to Jedidiah Morse, Hezekiah Niles, and the *Boston Post*, all attempts to fill the blank pages of his autobiography, he struggled against his own fear of history. He sought not personal glory in revolutionary chronicle, though he did feel slighted, but integrity and self-worth. His contretemps with Mercy Otis Warren over a few disparaging remarks about him in her history of the Revolution was turgid and shrill but owed less to advancing incapacity and overweaning pride than to his need for reassurance about the righteousness of his original purposes and the consistency of his ideas. If she were right, he had indeed been duped or foolish in his views of the French Revolution. Had this been true? It may seem so to the historian today, but to conclude on this note is to misunderstand Adams's passionate concern for the past. He wanted to set the record straight, not for adoring audiences or critical enemies but for himself. His life's work was to be a monument to personal and public independence; to his freedom from all considerations but those of virtue; to his country's freedom from tyranny; and, indissolubly bound to it, to his own mature identity. "I must think myself independent as long as I live," he wrote to Jefferson, "the feeling is essential to my existence." History, his history, his life's work, was too important to surrender.[24]

Proud, politic, old-fashioned Rufus King also made his peace with history. Bested in the senatorial debates of 1819–20 on Missouri, his advocacy of free soil used against him in his home state of New York, he sought some ground upon which to stand. On the edge of retirement, plagued by serious physical disabilities, he reconciled with history. "All that is the work of man," he told the Senate shortly before he left its halls, "is like him, imperfect. We probably enjoy a greater proportion of freedom and happiness than falls to the lot of other nations; and, because we desire yet more, we must be careful not to lose what we have, by hasty and partial alterations in our plan of government." It was a farewell thought as conservative as Jefferson's was progressive, yet, like Jefferson's, it reunited King with his real past and pronounced him content.[25]

Madison chose hope. Upon reception of a historical discourse from Dr. Daniel Drake, the promoter-historian of Cincinnati, Madison expressed delight: "Should the youth addressed [at Drake's lecture] and their successors, follow your advice, and their example be elsewhere imitated in noting from period to period the progress and changes of our country under the aspects adverted to . . . [it] will form a treasure of incalculable value to the Philosopher, the Lawgiver, and the Political Economist." Let the past, Madison pleaded, with all its errors, again teach the present: "Our history, short as it is, has already disclosed great errors sanctioned by great names . . . and it may be expected to throw new lights on problems still to be decided." There is a mixture of disgust and faith in these words, with faith finally victorious. The next year, 1836, he wrote another correspondent: "I am far however from desponding of the great political experiment in the hands of the American people. Much has already been gained in its favor, by the continued prosperity accompanying it through a period of so many years. Much may be expected from the progress and diffusion of political science." In his own careful preservation of historical documents and his encouragement to others to write histories of the revolutionary and constitutional dramas, he evidenced a personal commitment to the rebirth of history. By rediscovering the health of the republic from the study of its history, he reaffirmed his own worth.[26]

Before he died, Marshall, too, ceased to hide from history. To his confidant, fellow Supreme Court Justice Joseph Story, he jested, "I hope I shall live to read your lectures [on the history of the law]. They will form an exception to the plan of life I had formed for myself to be adopted after my retirement from office, that is to read nothing but novels and poetry." Close upon this reprieve for history came a full pardon, in a short note to a favorite grandson: "History is among the most essential departments of knowledge; and, to an American, the histories of England and of the United States are most instructive. Every man ought to be intimately acquainted with the history of his own country."[27]

Books about the Founding Fathers always end with the dying words of Adams, Jefferson, Madison, and Marshall. I will end this one with the last thoughts of a forgotten member of that generation. Despite the Republicans' victory in 1800, Philip Freneau remained mired in poverty and obscurity. He scribbled while his wife and daughters scratched a living from his dwindling patrimonial lands. Reaching old age, still largely unappreciated, he despaired. Epic poems planned in moments of euphoria went unfinished. The politics that had meant something to a younger Freneau ceased to energize his pen. Republican party triumphs only proved to him that his political opponents had not blocked his literary aspirations. His mind, like Rush's, strayed to the consolations of religion. "How feeble," he wrote in 1822, "are the strongest hands. How weak all human efforts prove." In spurts, his interest in publication revived—he produced a good number of patriotic poems during the War of 1812—but they never sold well. His recognition of the dismal conclusion of his personal history did not devastate him, however, for in his final years he gained strength from his perception that the larger history of his life—the historical events he shared with his generation—was a success. As he wrote to a new son-in-law, "The game [of political reaction] is over. You must pay respect and honor to America." As his own prospects faded, he was heartened by national improvements. Contemplating his younger friend DeWitt Clinton's canal in New York, Freneau wrote: "Nature herself will change her face / . . . And here behold a work progress, / Advancing through the wilderness, / A work, so recently began, / Where liberty enlightens man." And this message, read in the history of the new republic, comforted the stooped, aged poet-journalist. His last rhymes, never published, anticipated the winter of life with renewed faith: "These [memories] to the mind a thousand pleasures bring / And give to winter's frosts the smiles of spring."[28]

In their last years, the Founding Fathers doubted the value of their achievements. In moments of despair, rage, and resignation, they flirted with repudiation of their own history. A handful succumbed, but most did not. One might ask if they were being fair to themselves—if their self-censure was merited? As able as the revolutionary generation may have been in the eyes of its successors, it did not always fulfill its own stated goals. The revolutionaries did not find a way to place authority beyond the reach of corruption, unity beyond the danger of faction, or virtue beyond the reach of avarice and ambition. Nor did they discover a refuge for private life beyond the catcalls and importunities of the political forum.

Their goals were universal, but they accepted, bit by bit, a nationalistic reality. Their most eloquent spokesmen had yearned for a time when peace and reason would end the horrors of history; but history told them, in their dotage, that such a world was not to be. As old men, the revolutionaries remembered and regretted the lost illusions of their youth, manifest in their first, joyous plunge into American history.

With the cold breath of death upon their necks and the shield of history—their denial of death, their blazon of immortality—in pieces, the crisis of heart and soul that Ernest Becker describes was upon them. Their reply was not "unrepression," unthinking and unrestrained idealism. Nor was it a submission to the supernatural, a panicky search for cosmic release. Their reconciliation with their own history illustrated another option. They accepted death as the natural end to fulfilled lives. They bowed, gracefully, to their own humanity.[29]

CONCLUSION

Life Cycle and Historical Achievement

This book was introduced as a preliminary report on the relationship between life cycle and historical ideas among the revolutionary generation. It would therefore be unfair to offer any but the most tentative conclusions. Nevertheless, if the large topic merits further study, this brief inquiry should prove that the life-cycle approach can explain questions of intellectual history in novel and significant ways. Although grand estimates of each man should be left to closer students of their lives than I, it is proper here to judge the effectiveness with which they used history. From the perspective of modern scholarship, they were certainly not "objective," and for the most part they cannot be compared to the professional historian of today. From the standpoint of the psychology of human maturation and adjustment, however, they were brilliantly effective historians, for they built their vision of history into virtuous lives and careers.

As youths, they bound a new history together with the virtues of hope, will, purpose, and enthusiasm. Love and care succeeded loyalty and energy, as their chronicles of the 1780s were replaced by narratives and rationales they wrote in the 1790s. History was a mirror of ideals consciously held and unconsciously sought. When the survivors of the revolutionary generation doubted the veracity of history, they did so in the name of history's higher alter ego, virtue. At last, when they looked down upon history from the high place of old age, they wondered if their history—their achievements—could measure up to the integrity and responsibility they demanded of themselves. Strengthened by their self-evaluation, they found ways to face and accept past experience and ultimately to regain the wholeness of their lives before they died. These were the strengths their example bequeathed to later generations; strengths we, at this distance, can still clearly perceive.

A second conclusion is also in order. The history the revolutionary generation wrote and made focused upon the capacity of men to change the face of the world. Throughout their historical essays and asides ran the themes of individual power and genius, as well as virtue. To the mind of the eighteenth-century man, these were the ingredients, but not the sum total, of greatness. Then, as now, it is creativity that makes the difference between genuine greatness and great power, great intellect, and great virtue. Working outward from their historical vision to the reality of their life cycle, we may indulge ourselves in a moment of inquiry: did the revolutionary generation rise successfully to the challenge?

Each of life's stages poses its own difficulties, the resolution of which brings an individual to a higher plane of self-awareness and inner strength. Not every individual willingly faces these challenges, even among the Founding Fathers. That so many of the revolutionaries did resolve the successive crises of motivation and responsibility and were able, by combining personal and public concerns, to create a new republic is to their lasting credit and their successors' good fortune. This is what has made them great. From their personal point of view, the last of these crises, dealt with in the final chapter of this book, required the most severe effort. Out of its toils came a deeper understanding of human frailty and capacity. It was a final reckoning of selfhood that reduced pride to its rightful proportions but assured the revolutionaries that these proportions were estimable. Despair may induce an individual to devaluate a productive and eventful life. No one can blame the survivors of the Revolution for flirting with despondency, when the sacrifices and achievements of long careers appeared to be brought to naught by an uncaring public. In the main, the revolutionary generation did not surrender to its fears. Valuing their achievements fairly, learning to live with their opponents' criticisms and their own doubts, the young men of 1776 passed on their virtues to an entire people.

All human beings face the same sort of life-cycle challenges as the revolutionaries did, and all are parents to new generations of men and women. In the cycle of generations, the continual rebirth of human feelings and values, humanity finds the strength to explore itself and the world in greater and greater depth. But the revolutionary generation remains a special case, for the historian and for the inheritors of that Revolution. The founders of the republic, unlike most of us, left the impress of their passage through life's stages upon the institutions we still cherish. Their virtue and understanding, to paraphrase Erikson's more general pronouncement, left its "counterparts in the spirit of those human institutions which attempt to formalize and to safeguard such dealings." Their strengths became the strengths of the republic. "From the stages and virtues such individual dispositions as faith, judiciousness, moral purpose, technical efficiency, ideological devotion, ethical responsibility and detached sagacity flow into the life of institutions. Without them, institutions wilt."[1]

The lesson here is plain. It is a lesson that the Founding Fathers would have bid us commit to heart. Their institutions still live. History has not ended, and our fate is in our own hands. As Erikson has written: "I would posit a mutual activation and replenishment between the virtues emerging in

each individual life cycle and the strengths of human institutions." Jefferson and Adams would have said "amen" to
this, for they lived as though it were true. And their history—
the history they wrote and the history they made, their fusion
of personal life cycle with the birth and growth of public institutions—offers a concrete example of Erikson's proposi-
tion. The changes in revolutionary historical thought traced
in these chapters are the benchmarks by which one generation moved from youth to old age and the monuments they
left for those who would follow.[2]

Notes

INTRODUCTION

1. Erikson, *Childhood and Society*, rev. ed. (New York, 1963), 261–69; Erikson, "Identity Crisis in Autobiographical Perspective," in Erikson, *Life History and the Historical Moment* (New York, 1975), 21. A bibliography of Erikson's works appears in Robert Coles and John J. Fitzpatrick, "The Writings of Erik Erikson," *Psychohistory Review* 5 (1976): 42–46.

2. Erikson, *Childhood and Society*, 263; Theodore Lidz, *The Person, His Development through the Life Cycle* (New York, 1968), 81; Daniel J. Levinson et al., *The Seasons of a Man's Life* (New York, 1978), 317–40.

3. James Kirby Martin, *Men in Rebellion* (New Brunswick, N.J., 1973), 152–54, finds the mean age of revolutionary leaders only four years below that of Loyalist leaders; the "young revolutionaries" were, of course, at the lower end of the former scale.

4. On the concept of the "historical generation," see Karl Mannheim, "The Problem of Generations," in *Essays on the Sociology of Knowledge* (London, 1952), 276–322. There exist psychological studies of actual historical generations, such as Peter Loewenberg, "The Psychohistorical Origins of the Nazi Youth Cohort," *American Historical Review* 76 (1971): 1457–1502, or, closer in subject to the issues at hand, Philip J. Greven, Jr., *Four Generations: Population, Land, and Family in Colonial Andover, Massachusetts* (Ithaca, 1970), 279–81; Michael Paul Rogin, *Fathers and Children: Andrew Jackson and the Subjugation of the American Indian* (New York, 1976), 19–37; and George B. Forgie, *Patricide in the House Divided: A Psychological Interpretation of Lincoln and His Age* (New York, 1979). These are not based upon the concept of life cycle, however, but are variants of psychoanalysis. Carol Berkin, *Jonathan Sewall: Odyssey of an American Loyalist* (New

135

York, 1974), 8–9, suggests the utility of a "youth-young adulthood-maturity-old age" categorization.

5. Stanley Elkins and Eric McKitrick, "The Founding Fathers: Young Men of the Revolution," *Political Science Quarterly* 76 (1961): 203–6; David Hackett Fischer, *The Revolution of American Conservatism* (New York, 1969), xvi–xviii and ff.

6. Annie Kriegel, "Generational Difference: The History of an Idea," *Daedalus* 107 (Fall 1979): 29. Pauline Maier compares the generation of 1776 with the "old revolutionaries" in *The Old Revolutionaries: Political Lives in the Age of Samuel Adams* (New York, 1980), in which see 280–81 for the concept of apprenticeship.

7. On Lee, see Oliver P. Chitwood, *Richard Henry Lee: Statesman of the Revolution* (Morgantown, W.Va., 1967), 14; on Sherman, Roger S. Boardman, *Roger Sherman: Signer and Statesman* ([1938] New York, 1971), 53–54; on McKean, G. S. Rowe, *Thomas McKean: The Shaping of an American Republicanism* (Boulder, Colo., 1978), 17–29; on Boudinot, George A. Boyd, *Elias Boudinot: Patriot and Statesman* (Princeton, 1952), 20; on Belknap, George B. Kirsch, *Jeremy Belknap: A Biography* (New York, 1982), 7–10, 13–17, 29–31. As a mature individual, Belknap joined the patriot cause (Kirsch, *Belknap*, 51).

8. Robert V. Wells, *The Population of the British Colonies in America before 1776* (Princeton, 1975), 117, 269, 272, 284. In a study of this sort, one must be sensitive to the dangers of "trickle-down" history—the history that carelessly reads the ideas of elites for the aspirations of masses. See Jesse Lemisch, "The American Revolution Seen from the Bottom Up," in Barton Bernstein, ed., *Towards a New Past: Dissenting Essays in American History* (New York, 1968), 3–45. The remedy for this error has nothing to do with ideology. One must simply limit the generality of one's conclusions to the range of sources used in the study.

9. Erik Erikson, *Dimensions of a New Identity* (New York, 1974), 33.

10. Peter Shaw, *American Patriots and the Rituals of Revolution* (Cambridge, Mass., 1981), tackles the anomaly of the inflated rhetoric of the revolutionaries.

11. No scholar has questioned the fact that the revolutionary generation studied and used historical materials; see H. Trevor Colbourn, *The Lamp of Experience: Whig History and the Intellectual Origins of the American Revolution* (New York, 1974), 5 ff., and Henry Steele Commager, "Leadership in Eighteenth-Century America and Today," *Daedalus* 90 (Fall 1961): 655–56, among the many studies of the

revolutionaries' historical ideas. The question remains: how integral were the revolutionaries' historical ideas to their view of themselves? For some older revolutionaries, at certain times, historical arguments seem to have been an expected form of window-dressing; see Bernard Bailyn, *The Ideological Origins of the American Revolution* (Cambridge, Mass., 1967), 79–80. And not every member of my young men of 1776 turned to history to comfort, explain, prompt, and persuade. Recent biographies of William Paterson and Henry (Light Horse) Lee, to name two of this description, do show the rough outlines of life cycle and its challenges. If Paterson and Lee saw the law and the art of war as their own mirrors of the soul, their choices do not deny the validity of my thesis about other young men of 1776 who did think in historical terms.

CHAPTER ONE

1. Michael Kammen, *A Season of Youth: The American Revolution and the Historical Imagination* (New York, 1978), 198–201; Edmund Randolph, *History of Virginia* (1813), ed. Arthur H. Shaffer (Charlottesville, 1970), 199.

2. John Adams, *A Dissertation on the Canon and the Feudal Law* (1765), in Robert J. Taylor, ed., *The Papers of John Adams* (Cambridge, Mass., 1977–), 1: 113, 114, a draft of which appears on 1: 108–11.

3. James Wilson (untitled address, 1768), mentioned in Charles Page Smith, *James Wilson, Founding Father* (Chapel Hill, 1956), 35–36; Philip Freneau, *Rising Glory of America* (1772), in Freneau, *Poems Relating to the American Revolution* (New York, 1865), 8, 16.

4. Alexander Hamilton, *The Farmer Refuted* . . . (1775), in Harold C. Syrett, ed., *The Papers of Alexander Hamilton* (New York, 1961–), 1: 122; and see also Gerald Stourzh, *Alexander Hamilton and the Idea of Republican Government* (Stanford, 1970), 26–27.

5. Thomas Jefferson, *Summary View of the Rights of British America* (1774; London, 1775), 7–9, 18; Jefferson, "Declaration of the Causes of taking Up Arms" [fair copy for the committee] (1775), in *The Papers of Thomas Jefferson*, ed. Julian P. Boyd (Princeton, 1950–), 1: 199.

6. Lester H. Cohen, *The Revolutionary Histories* (Ithaca, N.Y., 1980), 52–53, 82–83, and ff., finds that the revolutionaries' histories were Puritan in their dedication and ethicality but wholly secular in their

view of cause and contingency. He does not restrict his remarks to the younger generation but does apply them to Ramsay and others among our "young men."

7. Colbourn, *Lamp of Experience*, 4, 185; Gordon Wood, *The Creation of the American Republic, 1776–1787* (New York, 1972), 30–31. The discovery that the youngest of the revolutionaries separated American history from English history does not dispute the Renaissance humanism recently discerned by J. G. A. Pocock, John Murrin, and others in American revolutionary ideology. No one would contend that Americans were literally faithful to their historical models, whether drawn from Burgh and the Commonwealth men, Harrington, or even Machiavelli. The severing of historical ties by Jefferson, Madison, Hamilton, and the rest did not mean that the lessons of the past, including those digested and reiterated by earlier scholars, were worthless. Insofar as Pocock can show the lines of development of Florentine civic thought, through the writings of mid-seventeenth-century English reformers, later "country" advocates, and, finally, our own revolutionaries, my argument does not undercut his. Virtue and corruption were indeed watchwords among this generation of young men, though they had consciously cut the historical ties which, in fact, brought these concepts into their culture. See Pocock, *The Machiavellian Moment: Florentine Political Thought and the Atlantic Republican Tradition* (Princeton, 1975), 506–52, and Murrin, "The Great Inversion, or Court versus Country," in Pocock, ed., *Three British Revolutions: 1641, 1688, 1776* (Princeton, 1980), 368–454.

8. Thomas Hutchinson, *The History . . . of Massachusetts Bay* (Boston, 1754), 1: xxix.

9. William Smith, Jr., *The History of New York* (1756; New York, 1814), 335.

10. James Logan, "Of the State of the British Plantations in America, A Memorial" (1732), ed. Joseph E. Johnson, *Pennsylvania Magazine of History and Biography* 60 (1936): 127; William Keith, *The History of the British Plantations in America*, Part I (London, 1738), 7; William Douglass, *A Summary, Historical and Political, of the British Settlements in North America*, (1748; Boston, 1755), 2: 17, 34; [Benjamin Franklin, with Richard Jackson], *An Historical Review of the Constitution and Government of Pennsylvania . . .* (London, 1759), 5.

11. Richard Bland, *An Inquiry into the Rights of the British Colonies* (1766; reprint, Williamsburg, 1922), 6; James Otis, Jr., *Rights of the British Colonies Asserted and Proved* (Boston, 1764), in Bernard Bailyn,

ed., *Pamphlets of the American Revolution* (Cambridge, Mass., 1965),
1: 429–30, 441; Patrick Henry to Benjamin Rush, 1775, recalled by
Rush in "Travels through Life" (1800), in *The Autobiography of Benjamin Rush*, ed. George W. Corner (Princeton, N.J., 1948), 111.

12. The debates were recorded in John Adams's Journal, June–
November 1774, reprinted in Edmund C. Burnett, ed., *Letters of
Members of the Continental Congress* (Washington, D.C., 1921–36), 1:
18–23. The delegates' views of American history reported by Adams
generally corresponded to ideas expressed by the delegates out of
doors. See, for example, on Lee, Chitwood, *Lee*, 83. Lee was as ardent an advocate of independence as Adams or Jefferson, yet, unlike
the latter two men, he had reached full emotional maturity before
the final crisis. He did not envision an independent American history, because his already established adult identity required no such
construction. On the cul-de-sac in historical protests based upon the
English constitution, see Pocock, *Machiavellian Moment*, 507–8.

13. Merrill Peterson, *Adams and Jefferson: A Revolutionary Dialogue*
(New York, 1978), 13–14.

14. Brackenridge's portion of "Rising Glory" (1771), in Daniel
Marder, ed., *A Hugh Henry Brackenridge Reader* (Pittsburgh, 1970), 58;
Erikson, *Childhood and Society*, 264–65, and generally, Erikson, *Identity: Youth and Crisis* (New York, 1968).

15. Erik Erikson, *Young Man Luther* (New York, 1958), 170–222.
On social control by parents, see Greven, *Four Generations*, 261–92;
Daniel Scott Smith, "Parental Power and Marriage Patterns; An
Analysis of Historical Trends in Hingham, Massachusetts," *Journal
of Marriage and the Family* 35 (1973): 419–28. On later maturation, see
Peter Laslett, "Age at Menarche in Europe since the Eighteenth Century," *Journal of Interdisciplinary History* 2 (Autumn 1971): 221–36; and
Edward Shorter, *The Making of the Modern Family*, 2d ed. (New York,
1977), 86 ff. On extended adolescence, see Ross W. Beales, Jr., "In
Search of the Historical Child: Miniature Adulthood and Youth in
Colonial New England," *American Quarterly* 27 (October 1975): 394;
N. Ray Hiner, "Adolescence in Eighteenth Century America," *History of Childhood Quarterly* 2 (1975): 254; and generally, Vivian C. Fox,
"Is Adolescence a Phenomenon of Modern Times?" *History of Childhood Quarterly* 5 (1977): 271–90.

16. Marvin Zahniser, ed., "Edward Rutledge to His Son, August
2, 1796," *South Carolina Historical Magazine* 64 (1963): 65–72; Peter
Shaw, *The Character of John Adams* (Chapel Hill, 1976), 65. The rite of
passage into politics during the Revolution was particularly tumul-

tuous, but the impact of the passage was not altered. See Charles S. Sydnor, *American Revolutionaries in the Making* (New York, 1975), 21–33, and Rhys Isaac, "Dramatizing the Ideology of Revolution: Popular Mobilization in Virginia," *William and Mary Quarterly*, 3d ser., 33 (1977): 357–85.

17. Myles Cooper, *The Patriots of North America* [1776], reprinted in *Magazine of History*, extra no. 27 (1914): 825.

18. Lyman H. Butterfield et al., eds. *The Diary and Autobiography of John Adams* (Cambridge, Mass., 1961), 3: 278–79. The author is indebted to Peter Shaw's *The Character of John Adams* for the thesis that Adams was, as his contemporaries understood, driven by ambition. Shaw's prose style is an inspiration in itself, which I am pleased to acknowledge.

19. James Thomas Flexner, *Young Hamilton: A Biography* (New York, 1978), 3–107.

20. Jefferson, *Autobiography of Thomas Jefferson* (1823), ed. Dumas Malone (New York, 1959), 21, 22, 24, 26; Merrill Peterson. *Thomas Jefferson and the New Nation* (New York, 1970), chap. 2; Fawn M. Brodie, *Thomas Jefferson: An Intimate History* (New York, 1974), 19–38; John Marshall, *An Autobiographical Sketch by John Marshall* (1827), ed. John Stokes Adams (Ann Arbor, 1937), 5.

21. John Adams, *Earliest Diary of John Adams*, ed. L. H. Butterfield (Cambridge, Mass., 1966), 71; Jefferson to Ebenezer Hazard, April 1775, Boyd, ed., *Papers of Jefferson*, 1: 164. See also editor's headnote to Adams-Sewall letters, 1766–67, in Taylor, ed., *Papers of John Adams*, 1: 176.

22. Timothy Pickering to John Clark, June 15, 1774, cited in Gerald Clarfield, *Timothy Pickering and the American Republic* (Pittsburgh, 1980), 16; James Madison to William Bradford, November 9, 1772, William T. Hutchinson and William M. E. Rachal, eds., *The Papers of James Madison* (Chicago and Charlottesville, 1962–), 1: 75; Bradford to Madison, May 27, 1773, *Papers of Madison*, 1: 86; James Wilson, *Considerations on the Nature and Extent of the Legislative Authority of the British Parliament* (Philadelphia, 1774). Alexander Hamilton's *Congress Vindicated . . .* (1774) and *Farmer Refuted* (1775) gained great applause among the revolutionaries; see John C. Miller, *Alexander Hamilton and the Growth of the New Nation* (New York, 1964), 10. On Gerry, see George Athan Billias, *Elbridge Gerry: Founding Father and Republican Statesman* (New York, 1976), 22.

23. Marvin Zahniser, *Charles Cotesworth Pinckney: Founding Father* (Chapel Hill, 1967), 14; Rush, "Travels," 46–47, 62, 76–77; and also

see David F. Hawke, *Benjamin Rush: Revolutionary Gadfly* (Indianapolis, 1971), 137–38.

24. John Adams, Diary entry for October 17, 1774, *Diary and Autobiography*, 2: 154; Bailyn, *Ideological Origins*, 26.

25. Philip Freneau, "Satires against the Tories," quoted in Jacob Axelrod, *Philip Freneau* (Austin, Tex., 1967), 32. On the parental imagery of the revolutionaries, see Edwin Burrows and Michael Wallace, "The American Revolution: The Ideology and Psychology of National Liberation," *Perspectives in American History* 6 (1972): 200–215; and Winthrop Jordan, "Familial Politics: Thomas·Paine and the Killing of the King 1776," *Journal of American History* 60 (September 1973): 294–308. Both of these are nontechnical adaptations of psychoanalytic theory; more vigorous application of this theory, stressing, naturally, the unresolved Oedipus complex, would lead to similar conclusions. Paranoia growing from fear of parental anger might result in "projection" of the kind described above. Closer to this approach is John J. Waters, "James Otis, Jr.: An Ambivalent Revolutionary," *History of Childhood Quarterly* 1 (1973): 142–50. Lawrence Henry Gipson, *The Coming of the Revolution* (New York, 1954), 232–33, among others, has defended the propriety of English behavior in the crisis.

The propaganda impact of the Declaration was not as great as the revolutionaries hoped—and I believe they suspected this would be the case. See Robert R. Palmer, "The Impact of the American Revolution Abroad," paper presented at the Fourth Symposium on the Bicentennial of the American Revolution, sponsored by the Library of Congress, May 8, 1975. With this in mind, we may propose less contrived and more compelling motives in the author of the document.

26. Richard M. Rollins, *The Long Journey of Noah Webster* (Philadelphia, 1980), 23–24; Erikson, "Identity Crisis in Autobiographical Perspective," 19.

27. Daniel J. Boorstin, *America and the Image of Europe* (New York, 1960), 66–78, discusses these methods of reshaping the past.

28. Brackenridge quoted in Daniel Marder, *Hugh Henry Brackenridge* (New York, 1967), 34–35; Rush, "Address to Subscribers to United Company for Promoting American Manufacturers," March 16, 1775, in Hawke, *Benjamin Rush*, 129; John Adams to Abigail Adams, July 3, 1776, in Burnett, ed., *Letters of the Members of the Continental Congress*, 1: 526.

29. William Bradford to James Madison, March 4, 1774, Hutchin-

son and Rachal, eds., *Papers of Madison*, 1: 109; Bradford to Madison, October 17, 1774, *Papers of Madison*, 1: 126; David Humphreys, *The Glory of America* (Philadelphia, 1783), *The Happiness of America* (Philadelphia, 1786), and other works extolled the "genius" of Americans. See also David Ramsay, *An Oration on the Advantages of American Independence* (Charleston, 1778), 5–6, 8. This concept was soon taken for granted here; on the "genius" of American law, see, for example, Charles Cotesworth Pinckney, John Marshall, and Elbridge Gerry to Talleyrand, April 3, 1798, in William Stinchcombe and Charles T. Cullen, eds., *Papers of John Marshall* (Chapel Hill, 1974–), 3: 447.

One might argue, following the work of Hans Kohut and others at the Chicago Institute for Psychoanalysis, that the extolling of "genius" by the revolutionaries was the mark of youthful narcissism. The vast self-confidence and self-absorption of the revolutionaries argues for this conclusion, but one must note that their direction of energy and care to public concerns was then a successful displacement of love object from self to commonwealth.

30. Douglass Adair, "Fame and the Founding Fathers," in H. Trevor Colbourn, ed., *Fame and the Founding Fathers: Essays by Douglass Adair* (New York, 1974), 7, 11; Jay to McDougall, April 27, 1776, in Richard B. Morris, *John Jay: The Making of A Revolutionary* (New York, 1976), 263.

31. Erik Erikson, *Identity and the Life Cycle, Psychological Issues* 1 (1959): 89.

32. John M. Murrin, "Anglicization and Identity: The Colonial Experience, the Revolution, and the Dilemma of American Nationalism," paper presented at the Organization of American Historians, Denver, Colorado, April 1974, traces the problems historians have had with the concept of revolutionary nationalism. Any ideology, and "nationalism" is no exception, is an attempt to make sense of reality. As with all powerful intellectual movements, the invention of a new ideology takes on a life of its own and motivates new forms of action. Erikson has written: "In some periods of his history, and in some phases of his life cycle, man needs (until we invent something better) a new ideological orientation as surely and as sorely as he must have air and food. . . . The total perspective created by ideological simplification reveals its strength by the dominance it exerts on the seeming logic of historical events, and by its influence on the identity formation of individuals" (*Young Man Luther*, 22). One may view the creation of a separate American history as "ideological simplification."

CHAPTER TWO

1. A succinct statement of these beliefs is Douglass Adair, "Experience Must Be Our Only Guide: History, Democratic Theory, and the United States Constitution" (1966), in Colbourn, ed., *Fame and the Founding Fathers*, 107–23, but see also Bailyn, *Ideological Origins*, 85, and Stow Persons, "Cyclical Theory of History in Eighteenth-Century America," *American Quarterly* 5 (April 1954): 147–67.

2. Although the internal dynamics of state and confederation politics are at this publishing very controversial issues for historians, no one can doubt the tumultuousness of this era. See Jack N. Rakove, *The Beginnings of National Politics: An Interpretive History of the Continental Congress* (New York, 1979), and Jackson T. Main, *Political Parties before the Constitution* (Chapel Hill, 1973), for summaries of the divisive issues.

3. Erikson, *Childhood and Society*, 264–66; Levinson, *Seasons of a Man's Life*, 71–73.

4. Jay to Egbert Benson, September 12, 1783, Henry P. Johnston, ed., *Papers and Public Correspondence of John Jay* (New York, 1890–93), 3: 75; Edward Rutledge to Jay, November 12, 1786, *Correspondence of Jay*, 3: 217; Marshall, *Autobiographical Sketch*, 8; Jefferson, *Autobiography*, 88–89; Wood, *Creation of the American Republic*, 397.

5. John Adams, "Memorial to their High Mightinesses, the States General . . . (1781), in Charles Francis Adams, ed., *Life and Works of John Adams* (Boston 1851–56), 7: 397; Joel Barlow, *Address to the Society of the Cincinnati, July 4th, 1787*, in Hezekiah Niles, ed., *Principles and Acts of the Revolution in America* (Baltimore, 1822), 146; David Ramsay, *History of the Revolution of South Carolina from a British Province to an Independent State*, 2 vols. (Philadelphia, 1784–85), dedication.

6. Ramsay, *History*, 1: 7, 12, 19, 69, 126, 217, 2: 176, 196, 247; Ramsay to Benjamin Rush, February 11, 1786, in Robert L. Brunhouse, ed., "David Ramsay, 1749–1815, Selections from His Writings," *Transactions of the American Philosophical Society*, n.s., 55 (1965): pt. 4, 98.

7. Webster, *A Collection of Essays, on . . . Moral, Political, Historical, and Literary Subjects* (Boston, 1790), 100; Humphreys, *An Oration on the Political Situation . . . in the Year 1789* (1789), in William K. Bottoroff, ed., *Miscellaneous Works of David Humphreys*, (1804; Gainesville, Fla., 1968) 340; Humphreys et al., *The Anarchiad: A New England Poem* (New Haven, 1787), iv, 1, 2–7, 23–24, 61.

8. Joel Barlow, *An Oration delivered at . . . Hartford . . . at the Society*

of the Cincinnati . . . 4th of July, 1787 (Hartford, 1787), 4.

9. Madison to Washington, April 16, 1787, Hutchinson and Rachal, eds., *Papers of Madison*, 10: 383. On the persistence of familial language of authority, see Philip Greven, *The Protestant Temperament: Patterns of Child-Rearing, Religious Experience, and the Self in Early America* (New York, 1977), 353, 359; and Wood, *Creation of the American Republic*, 478–79. Excessive attempts to impose order (for example, the Cincinnati) were resisted, however. See Charles Royster, *A Revolutionary People at War: The Continental Army and American Character, 1775–1783* (Chapel Hill, 1979), chap. 8.

10. Randolph to Washington, November 24, 1786, in Moncure D. Conway, *Omitted Chapters of History . . . in the Life and Papers of Edmund Randolph* (New York, 1888), 60; Washington to Randolph, upon receiving a nomination to the federal Constitutional Convention, December 21, 1786, John C. Fitzpatrick, ed., *The Writings of George Washington*, (Washington, D.C., 1939), 24: 120.

11. Brodie, *Jefferson*, 207; Billias, *Gerry*, 147; Pinckney to James Madison, March 28, 1789, Hutchinson and Rachal, eds., *Papers of Madison*, 12: 35; Levinson, *Seasons of a Man's Life*, 73–74; Flexner, *Hamilton*, 429–35.

12. Hugh Henry Brackenridge, *Modern Chivalry* (1784–85), Part I, ed. Claude M. Newlin (New York, 1962), 76–77; Joel Barlow to Noah Webster, January 30, 1779, in Charles B. Todd, *The Life and Letters of Joel Barlow* (New York, 1886), 18; Noah Webster, *A Grammatical Institute of the English Language* (Hartford, 1785), 13–14. Hope and disappointment were mingled, for these writers had expected the Revolution to stimulate the arts. See Joseph J. Ellis, *After the Revolution* (New York, 1979), 29.

13. Jay to John Adams, May 4, 1786, Johnston, ed., *Correspondence of Jay*, 3: 194; Adams to King, June 14, 1786, quoted in Robert Ernst, *Rufus King: American Federalist* (Chapel Hill, 1968), 68.

14. Ramsay to Benjamin Rush, April 8, 1777, Brunhouse, ed., "Ramsay, Selections," 54. The important point here is not that the young became federalists while the old joined the antifederalist ranks (though some age dispersion did appear) but that the old revolutionaries clung to comparative history while the younger revolutionaries were freed (or compelled) to work out the implications of their own, earlier, separation of American history from its precursors. The young federalists were encouraged by their discovery of our historical incomparability to plunge into thorough constitutional reform. Young antifederalists were the first of their faction to grasp the

force of the new history, and they tried to turn it to their own advantage.

15. Timothy Dwight, "Columbia, A Song," *American Museum* 3 (June 1787): 484, but compare his dismal conclusions in *America; or, A Poem on the Settlement of the British Colonies* (New Haven, 1780). Joel Barlow, *The Vision of Columbus* (1787), 5th ed. (Paris, 1798), 9: 264, 8: 215–16; Barlow, *Oration . . . at . . . Hartford*, 6; Benjamin Rush, *Thoughts upon the Mode of Education . . .* (Philadelphia, 1786), quoted in Allen O. Hansen, *Liberalism and American Education* (New York, 1926), 49–57; Rush to Jeremy Belknap, June 6, 1791, Lyman H. Butterfield, ed., *The Letters of Benjamin Rush* (Princeton, 1951) 1: 583.

16. Thomas Jefferson, *Notes on the State of Virginia* (1781–87), ed. William Peden (Chapel Hill, 1953), 117–20, 148, 192.

17. John Adams, *Defense of the Constitutions of the . . . United States*, 3 vols. (London, 1787), 1: ii, xxv. A different reading of the *Defense* is found in Shaw, *Character of John Adams*, 206–24.

18. Alexander Hamilton, "The Continentalist" (1782), Syrett, ed., *Papers of Hamilton*, 3: 103.

19. James Madison to the Constitutional Convention, June 21, 1787; Wilson to the convention, June 20, 1787; Madison to the convention, August 13, 1787; Charles Pinckney to the convention, June 25, 1787, in Max Farrand, ed., *The Records of the Federal Convention of 1787*, 4 vols., rev. ed. (New Haven, 1937), 1: 356–57, 337, 343, 2: 268–69, 1: 398–401.

20. Noah Webster, *An Examination into the Leading Principles of the Federal Constitution* (1787), in Paul L. Ford, ed., *Pamphlets on the Constitution of the United States* (New York, 1888), 29–35. An egocentric nationalistic history was not, of course, the only expression of this longing for an escape from the toils of the cyclical theory of history. A second line of reasoning lay in the lexicography of a unique American language. This effort was led by Webster. The attempt to fashion a superior and incorruptible republican educational system also grew from the fear of earlier republics' fates, and Jefferson and Rush, among other young revolutionaries, would assume the direction of this project in later years.

21. John Jay, *Address to the People of the State of New York on the Subject of the Constitution* (1787), in Ford, ed., *Pamphlets*, 70; John Jay, *Address to the People of the State of New York* (1788), in Johnston, ed., *Correspondence of Jay*, 3: 296.

22. [Madison and Hamilton], *Federalist No. 18, The Federalist Papers*, ed. Clinton Rossiter (New York, 1961), 122–28.

23. Elbridge Gerry, *Observations on the New Constitution* . . . (Boston, 1788), 3–4.

24. Theodore Sedgwick to Massachusetts ratification convention, January 14, 1788; Fisher Ames to convention, January 15, 1788, Rufus King to convention, January 15, 1788, in Jonathan Elliot, ed., *Debates on the Constitution*, (Washington, D.C., 1836), 2: 4, 8, 10, 12, 18, 19, 20.

25. Rufus King to Massachusetts convention, January 21, 1788; John Gorham to convention, January 21, 1788, *Debates on the Constitution*, 2: 55, 68–69.

26. Fisher Ames to Massachusetts convention, January 25, 1788; John Nason to convention, February 1, 1788, *Debates on the Constitution*, 2: 101, 135–37.

27. James Wilson to Pennsylvania ratification convention, November 26, 1787, *Debates on the Constitution*, 2: 422–23.

28. Patrick Henry to Virginia ratification convention, June 5, 1788, *Debates on the Constitution*, 3: 45–46, 53, 62. Was age, and with it, differences in stage of life, a cause of different views of the Constitution? The latest essay on the subject, Maier's *Old Revolutionaries*, 285–92, finds that different generations had different perspectives. She focuses on the Virginia ratification debates between Henry and Randolph to make her point. Although she does not use the life-cycle theory explicitly here, her argument does support my conclusions.

29. Edmund Randolph to Virginia convention, June 6, 1788, *Debates on the Constitution*, 3: 66, 69, 75.

30. James Madison to Virginia convention, June 6–7, 1788, *Debates on the Constitution*, 3: 87, 92, 129–32.

31. Patrick Henry to Virginia convention, June 7, 9, 1788, *Debates on the Constitution*, 3: 143, 160, 162, 185.

32. James Wilson, "Address," *Account of the Grand Federal Procession, Philadelphia, July 4, 1788* (Philadelphia, 1788), 14; Wilson, *On the Study of Law in the United States* (1790–91 lectures), in Randolph G. Adams, ed., *Selected Political Essays of James Wilson* (New York, 1930), 186; also see Smith, *James Wilson*, 270–77.

33. George Nicholas to Madison, November 2, 1789, Hutchinson and Rachal, eds., *Papers of Madison*, 12: 445–46.

34. Hamilton quoted in Stourzh, *Hamilton and the Idea of Republican Government*, 172; see also Felix Gilbert, *To the Farewell Address: The Beginnings of American Foreign Policy* (New York, 1965), 127–34.

35. Wilson to Pennsylvania convention, December 12, 1787, quoted

in Smith, *James Wilson*, 277; see also Adrienne Koch, *Jefferson and Madison: The Great Collaboration* (New York, 1964), 141–42, Jefferson, *Autobiography*, 86–87, and Peter C. Hoffer, "The Constitutional Crisis and the Rise of a Nationalistic View of History in America, 1785–1789," *New York History* 52 (July 1971): 305–23.

CHAPTER THREE

1. Lawrence Cremin, *American Education: The Colonial Experience, 1607–1783* (New York, 1970), 568.

2. On the educational aspirations of this generation there can be no question of sincerity or commitment. For example, Jefferson to J. Barrister, October 15, 1785, in E. W. Knight, ed., *A Documentary History of Education in the South before 1860*, (Chapel Hill, 1950), 2: 5–6; Roy J. Honeywell, *The Educational Work of Thomas Jefferson* (New York, 1964), 140; and Jefferson, *Notes on the State of Virginia*, 206. Unfortunately, many of their schemes failed. See Linda K. Kerber, *Women of the Republic: Intellect and Ideology in Revolutionary America* (Chapel Hill, 1980), 185–232; and Joseph F. Kett, *Rites of Passage: Adolescence in America, 1790 to the Present* (New York, 1977), chap. 2.

3. Erikson, *Childhood and Society*, 266–68; Levinson, *Seasons of a Man's Life*, 253–54.

4. Barlow to Noah Webster, August 31, 1782, in Todd, *Barlow*, 42; Ramsay to Belknap, August 11, 1792, in Brunhouse, ed., "Ramsay, Selections," 133; Barlow, Remarks on Reception of the Letter to the *Centinel*, 1800 [?], in Todd, *Barlow*, 169; John Marshall "To A Freeholder," October 2, 1798, Stinchcombe and Cullen, eds., *Papers of Marshall*, 3: 504.

5. John Quincy Adams reflecting on the 1790s in *An Eulogy on the Life and Character of James Monroe* (Boston, 1831), 6, 47–49. On the effect of the French Revolution upon American political behavior, see Paul Goodman, "The First American Party System," in William N. Chambers and Walter D. Burnham, eds., *The American Party Systems* (New York, 1967), 74–75. Richard B. Morris, *The Emerging Nations and the American Revolution* (New York, 1970), 68–73, and Robert R. Palmer, *The Age of Democratic Revolution, Part I: The Challenge* (Princeton, 1959), 487ff., describe the French revolutionary fervor here. On the general influence of "revolutionary romanticism" in the 1790s, see Henry F. May, *The Enlightenment in America* (New York, 1976), 223–51.

6. Michael Kammen, *People of Paradox: An Inquiry Concerning the*

Origins of American Civilization (New York, 1973), 97–102. Just now (1983) the origin of these biformities is controversial. Scholars recently have identified Florentine civic humanists, English Whig constitutional reformers and reactionary Tories, Scottish moral philosophers (among whom sentimentalists wrestled with rationalists), country party spokesmen, and radical commonwealthmen as the source of our revolutionary ideas. For the roll, see Daniel Walker Howe, "European Sources of Political Ideas in Jeffersonian America," *Reviews in American History* 10 (1982): 28–44.

7. Jefferson to Madison, August 28, 1789, September 6, 1789, Hutchinson and Rachal, eds., *Papers of Madison*, 12: 361, 382–87; Hugh Henry Brackenridge, "Fourth of July Oration, 1793," in Marder, *Brackenridge*, 52.

8. [James Madison], *National Gazette*, September 26, 1792; [Philip Freneau], *National Gazette*, November 14, 1791. On Freneau's fear of monarchical forces, a very common emotion among the Francophiles, see Philip M. Marsh, *The Works of Philip Freneau: A Critical Study* (Metuchen, N.J., 1968), 66ff.

9. Jefferson to D'Invernois, February 6, 1795, Andrew Lipscomb and A. E. Bergh, eds., *Writings of Thomas Jefferson* (Washington, D.C., 1903), 9: 300; Jefferson to Barlow, December 10, 1807, *Writings of Jefferson*, 11: 400–401. Robert R. Palmer has judged 1795 as a turning point for American sympathy for France; thereafter popular support for France declined (*The Age of Democratic Revolution, II: The Struggle* [Princeton, 1964], 538, 540). Jefferson remained optimistic about French prospects well into the 1790s, possibly because he was getting French news months late and usually refused to believe the worst about the French leaders; see Dumas Malone, *Jefferson and the Ordeal of Liberty* (Boston, 1962), 38ff.

10. Jefferson to Edmund Pendleton, July 24, 1791, Lipscomb and Bergh, eds., *Writings of Jefferson*, 18: 187.

11. [Freneau], *National Gazette*, September 14, 1793; [Madison], *National Gazette*, September 26, 1793; Edmund Randolph, *A Vindication of Mr. Randolph's Resignation* (1795), ed. P. V. Daniel, Jr. (Richmond, 1855), 74. On the larger Jay Treaty debate, see Jerald A. Combs, *The Jay Treaty: Political Battleground of the Founding Fathers* (Berkeley, 1970), 159–88.

12. This view of the novelty and "modernity" of Republican opposition is traced in William N. Chambers, *Political Parties in the New Nation* (New York, 1963). James Morton Smith, *Freedom's Fetters: The*

Alien and Sedition Acts and American Civil Liberties, rev. ed. (Ithaca, 1963), 112–55, documents the fury of the Republicans.

13. George Nicholas, *A Letter . . . On the Alien and Sedition Acts* (Philadelphia, 1799), 4, 20, 36–37; see also St. George Tucker, *A Letter . . . Respecting the Alien and Sedition Acts* (n.p., 1798), 12–26, 29; and *The Speech of Edward Livingston on . . . the Alien and Sedition Acts* (Philadelphia, 1798), 4–5, 8, 16.

14. [James Madison], *Report of the Resolution of the Virginia House on the Alien and Sedition Acts* (1799–1800), Gaillard Hunt, ed., *The Writings of James Madison* (New York, 1900–1910), 6: 348, 352. See also Madison's *Address of the General Assembly to the People . . . of Virginia, Writings of Madison*, 6: 338.

15. [Thomas Jefferson], "Draft of Kentucky Resolutions," in Paul L. Ford, ed., *The Writings of Thomas Jefferson*, (New York, 1892–99), 7: 288–309; Jefferson to Elbridge Gerry, March 29, 1801, Lipscomb and Bergh, eds., *Writings of Jefferson*, 10: 252. On the authorship and transmission of the Resolutions, see Koch, *Jefferson and Madison*, 174–211, and James Morton Smith, "The Grass Roots Origins of the Kentucky Resolutions," *William and Mary Quarterly*, 3d ser., 27 (1970): 221–45.

16. This impression cannot be fully documented here, though one or two examples may make the argument clearer. James Callender's animadversions upon the Adams administration's sponsorship of the seditious libel law took the form of a history of the Federalists' adoration of Britain and aristocracy, but the historical material in his *Prospect Before Us* (1800) was not meant to express any attachment to the past. Perhaps this is because Callender, like Burk and Duane, was an immigrant. On the other hand, William Branch Giles was a native-born Virginian, and though the same age as Callender, had roots in Virginia's economic and social elite and therefore her history. Yet when he stood in the Congress to attack the same sedition bill, he, too, refused to attach himself to the past. He did use historical arguments to prove the royalist implications of the proposed legislation, but his examples were only examples—not pieces of his own experience recast and pressed upon his audience as lessons. The reason is simply that, unlike Madison and Jefferson, he had not reached the stage of his own life where personal experience cried for regeneration. On Callender and the crisis, see Smith, *Freedom's Fetters*, 336 ff. On Giles, see Dice Robins Anderson, *William Branch Giles* (Menasha, Wisc., 1914), 66–67. How different—protective and pro-

prietary—was the view Giles took of the same events in 1827. By then, the episode was part of a historical lesson which he wished to teach to a younger generation. On the 1827 reminiscence, see Anderson, *Giles*, 70–71.

17. Ames to William Tudor, July 12, 1789, in Winfred E. A. Bernhard, *Fisher Ames: Federalist and Statesman, 1758–1808* (Chapel Hill, 1965), 101.

18. Pickering to Timothy Williams, in Octavius Pickering and Charles W. Upham, *The Life of Timothy Pickering*, 4 vols. (Boston, 1868–73), 3: 181; Fisher Ames, *An Oration on . . . General George Washington . . . 8th of February, 1800* (Boston, 1800), 17–18. A recounting of the ideological pronouncements of these party leaders, beginning with their renunciation of parties, is Richard J. Buel, Jr., *Securing the Revolution: Ideology in American Politics, 1789–1815* (Ithaca, N.Y., 1972).

19. David Humphreys to Washington, March 24, 1793, Frank L. Humphreys, ed., *Life and Times of David Humphreys*, 2 vols. (New York, 1917), 2: 170–73; Gouverneur Morris to Uriah Tracy, January 5, 1804, Anne C. Morris, ed., *Diary and Letters of Gouverneur Morris*, 2 vols. (New York, 1888), 2: 451–52; John Marshall, *The Life of George Washington*, 5 vols. (Richmond, 1804–7), 5: 34, 86–89.

20. [John Fenno], "French Influence," *Gazette of the United States*, May 12–27, 1797; Fisher Ames, "Foreign Politics No. 1" (1801), in Seth Ames, ed., *The Works of Fisher Ames*, 2 vols. (Boston, 1854), 2: 207–8.

21. Morris to Washington, February 14, 1793, Morris, ed., *Diary and Letters of Morris*, 2: 41; Hamilton to Washington, September 15, 1790, Syrett, ed., *Papers of Hamilton*, 7: 30, 43; Hamilton to Jefferson, March 1793, Henry Cabot Lodge, ed., *Works of Alexander Hamilton*, 12 vols. (New York, 1904), 4: 351–75.

22. John Jay to Timothy Pickering, August 17, 1795, in *Life of Pickering*, 3: 198; Pickering to C. C. Pinckney, September 14, 1796, in *Life of Pinckney*, 3: 345; John Marshall to Charles Lee, October 25, 1797, Stinchcombe and Cullen, eds., *Papers of Marshall*, 3: 251.

23. Ames to Rufus King, October 27, 1801, Charles R. King, ed., *Life and Correspondence of Rufus King*, 4 vols. (New York, 1897), 4: 5.

24. The difference between Whig history and "evangelistic history" was the centrality of the deity in the latter; see Alan Heimert, *Religion and the American Mind: From the Great Awakening to the Revolution* (Cambridge, Mass., 1966), 387–89, 395–96. In different terms, older, more orthodox Calvinist divines in New England had made the same point about American history's divergence from other na-

tions'; see Peter Gay, *A Loss of Mastery: Puritan Historians in Colonial America* (Berkeley, 1966), 25, 116–17, and May, *Enlightenment in America*, 189–90. Dwight's contributions to the older Federalist historical corpus are discussed on 52–53 and 95–96.

25. Jedidiah Morse, *American Universal Geography* (New Haven, 1794), 1: 239–40, 253, 263–68, 291, 384, 432, 442—a wealth of references to history in a book that paid more than lip service to inculcating conservative values in young readers. See also Morse, *The Present Situation* (Boston, 1795), 14, and Morse, *A Sermon . . . May 9th, 1798* (Boston, 1798), 19.

26. John Adams, *Discourses on Davila* (1790), in Adams, ed., *Life and Works of John Adams*, 6: 276–77, 273. Both Adams's comprehension of the French reformers' purpose and his own ideological consistency in the early 1790s have been questioned. Edward Handler, *America and Europe in the Political Thought of John Adams* (Cambridge, 1964), chap. 3, argues that Adams misunderstood the French revolt. John R. Howe, Jr., *The Changing Political Thought of John Adams* (Princeton, 1966), finds *Davila* a midpoint between Adams's early fear of aristocracy and his later appreciation of the role of aristocratic symbols. Older scholarship found Adams simply a consistent advocate of mixed government; see Adrienne Koch, ed., *Adams and Jefferson: Posterity Must Judge* (Chicago, 1963), 49ff. "Adams's attitude toward the French revolution was strikingly similar to that of Burke," according to Zoltan Haraszti, *John Adams and the Prophets of Progress* (Cambridge, Mass., 1954), 21, but, unlike Burke, Adams was friendly to the French when they incorporated parts of the *Defense* into their constitution. Burke's *Reflections* was published at the same time as the *Davila* though both men made their opinion of the French crisis known earlier.

27. Webster to Jefferson, December 12, 1790, in Harry R. Warfel, ed., *Letters of Noah Webster* (New York, 1953), 88–89; Webster, *Address to the Public*, July 19, 1796, in *Letters of Webster*, 138. On Federalist xenophobia, see Smith, *Freedom's Fetters*, 22–34.

28. David Osgood, *A Discourse, Delivered February 19, 1975 . . .* (Boston, 1795), 11; David Humphreys, *Poem on the Industry of the United States of America* (1802), in *Miscellaneous Works*, 111; Timothy Dwight, *Greenfield Hill* (1794), in William J. McTaggert and William K. Bottoroff, eds., *The Major Poems of Timothy Dwight* (Gainesville, Fla., 1969), 385–96.

29. Hamilton, "The Examination No. VIII" (1802), in Syrett, ed., *Papers of Hamilton*, 25: 496.

30. Ames to George Minot, May 3, 1789, Ames, ed., *Works of Fisher Ames*, 1: 34. Jay Fliegelman, *Prodigals and Pilgrims: The American Revolution Against Patriarchal Authority, 1750–1800* (Cambridge, Eng., 1982), 198, finds "Washington not only brought the new world to life" for his admirers, but "he sealed it off from corruption, formed its character by the force of his virtuous example, and brought his nation to manhood." For this, he was not revered as a stern patriarch, but as a gentle, loving father and friend (199–200). One ought to note that this view of Washington was not universally held, for it represented a conception of parenthood congenial to the "friends of order" only. The older Jeffersonians do not appear in Fliegelman's citations because they had other notions of generativity.

31. Hamilton to Washington, May 19, 1798, Syrett, ed., *Papers of Hamilton*, 21: 466–68.

32. Gerry to ————, April 13, 1801, quoted in Billias, *Gerry*, 304.

33. David Ramsay, *An Oration, . . . On the Fourth of July, 1794* (Charleston, 1794), 26.

CHAPTER FOUR

1. Retirement in the nineteenth century's opening decades, especially among active agriculturalists like Jefferson and Madison, did not mean the end of employment. On different notions of retirement, see Kurt W. Back, "The Ambiguity of Retirement," in Ewald W. Busse and Eric Pfeiffer, eds., *Behavior and Adaptation in Late Life* (Boston, 1969), 93–114.

2. Adams to Benjamin Rush, June 20, 1808, in John A. Schutz and Douglass Adair, eds., *The Spur of Fame: Dialogues of John Adams and Benjamin Rush, 1805–1813* (San Marino, Ca., 1966), 110; Adams to Cunningham, September 27, 1808, E. M. Cunningham, ed., *Correspondence between . . . John Adams and . . . William Cunningham* (Boston, 1823), 30; John Marshall to Rufus King, May 5, 1802, King, ed., *Life and Correspondence of Rufus King*, 4: 118; Benjamin Rush to Adams, August 14, 1805, in Schutz and Adair, eds., *The Spur of Fame*, 32.

3. Adams to Jefferson, July 9, 1813, Lipscomb and Bergh, eds., *Writings of Jefferson*, 13: 304; Adams to McKean, August 31, 1813, Adams, ed., *Life and Works of John Adams*, 10: 62; Jefferson to Barlow, April 16, 1811, Lipscomb and Bergh, eds., *Writings of Jefferson*, 13: 44.

4. Hamilton, *Letter . . . Concerning the Public Conduct and Character*

of John Adams (October 1800) in Syrett, ed., *Papers of Hamilton*, 25: 186–88, 193, 224, 229, 233–34; Hamilton, "Examination, No. IX" (1802), *Papers*, 25: 501.

5. Ames to Oliver Wolcott, March 9, 1803, quoted in Bernhard, *Fisher Ames*, 338–39; Ames to George Cabot, February 1804, reported by Cabot to Pickering, February 14, 1804, quoted in Bernhard, *Fisher Ames*, 341; Ames, *The Danger of American Liberty* (1805), in Ames, ed., *Works of Fisher Ames*, 2: 345–46.

6. Rush to John Adams, February 19, 1805, Butterfield, ed., *Letters of Benjamin Rush*, 2: 891; Rush to James McHenry, August 12, 1800, *Letters Rush*, 2: 819; Rush, to Jefferson, March 15, 1813, *Letters of Rush*, 2: 1189; Rush, "Travels," 117; Rush to Adams, November 17, 1812, *Letters of Rush*, 2: 1166.

7. On the patriotic historical panegyrics of the postwar generation, see Robert P. Hay, "The Glorious Departure of the American Patriarchs: Contemporary Reactions to the Deaths of Jefferson and Adams," *Journal of Southern History*, 35 (1969): 543–55, and George H. Callcott, *History in the United States, 1800–1860* (Baltimore, 1970).

8. Gouverneur Morris, "Inaugural Address, September 4, 1816," *Collections of the New York Historical Society for the Year 1821* (New York, 1821), 28; John Jay to Morris, October 28, 1816, Johnston, ed., *Correspondence of Jay*, 4: 394; Jay to McDougall, April 27, 1776, in Morris, *John Jay*, 263; Jay to Jedediah Morse, February 28, 1797, *Correspondence of Jay*, 4: 224; Jay to Judge Peters, December 26, 1820, *Correspondence of Jay*, 4: 436–37.

9. Marshall to Joseph Delaplaine, March 22, 1818, Irwin S. Rhodes, ed., *Papers of John Marshall: A Descriptive Calendar*, 2 vols. (Norman, Okla., 1969), 2: 135; Marshall to Joseph Story, December 9, 1823, in John E. Oster, ed., *The Political and Economic Doctrines of John Marshall* (New York, 1914), 120–21; Marshall to Charles Carter, January 29, 1832, *Doctrines of Marshall*, 48; Marshall to Pickering, March 20, 1826, *Doctrines of Marshall*, 95. The effect of Marshall's Federalism on his history is traced in William Smith, *History as Argument* (The Hague, 1965), 191ff. Contemporary response is recorded in Albert Beveridge, *Life of John Marshall*, 4 vols. (New York, 1919), 3: 223–73.

10. Rufus King to Christopher Gore, May 8, 1816, quoted in Ernst, *King*, 350; Rufus King to T. Coleman, July 1818, King, ed., *Life and Correspondence of Rufus King*, 6: 157–58.

11. Jefferson to William Johnson, March 4, 1823, Lipscomb and Bergh, eds., *Writings of Jefferson*, 15: 420; Jefferson, Introduction [1818], *The Complete 'Anas' of Thomas Jefferson*, ed. Franklin B. Sawvel (1903;

New York, 1970), 24–26, 30, 35, 38; Jefferson to Francis Gilmer, November 25, 1823, Richard Beale Davis, ed., *Correspondence of Thomas Jefferson and Francis Walker Gilmer, 1814–1826* (Columbia, S.C., 1946), 77.

12. Loss of control and consequent soul-searching over the meaning of one's life is discussed in L. David Levi, Helm Stierlin, and Robert J. Savard, "Fathers and Sons: The Interlocking Crises of Integrity and Identity," *Psychiatry* 35 (1972): 48–56.

13. Erikson, *Childhood and Society*, 268–69; see also Douglas C. Kimmel, *Adulthood and Aging: An Interdisciplinary Development View* (New York, 1974), 343–90. On Jefferson, see Brodie, *Jefferson*, 601, and on Madison, Koch, *Jefferson and Madison*, 286. Richard Sennett explains the public masks eighteenth-century men wore in *The Fall of Public Man* (New York, 1977), 47–122.

14. John Adams to Jefferson, July 1813, Lipscomb and Bergh, eds., *Writings of Jefferson*, 13: 301; Jefferson to Josephus B. Stuart, May 10, 1817, *Writings*, 15: 113.

15. Humphreys [June 27, 1813], "On the Necessity of State and Self Defense; Address to the Inhabitants of Connecticut," in Humphreys, ed., *Life and Times of David Humphreys*, 2: 394, 396; David Hackett Fischer, *Growing Old in America*, rev. ed. (New York, 1977), 68; Noah Webster, *Letters to a Young Gentleman, Concerning his Education* (New Haven, 1823), passim; Webster to Governor John Brooks of Massachusetts, May 1819, Warfel, ed., *Letters of Webster*, 396–98.

16. Webster, *An American Dictionary of the English Language* (New York, 1828), v. My account follows Rollins, *Long Journey of Noah Webster*, 107–43.

17. Ernest Becker, *The Denial of Death* (New York, 1973), ix, 5, 15, 22. On Pickering's denial of death, see Clarfield, *Pickering*, 263.

18. Humphreys, "A Discourse upon Agriculture, New Haven, 1816," in Humphreys, ed., *Life and Times of David Humphreys*, 2: 424; Timothy Dwight, *Travels in New England and New York* [1817], ed. Barbara Miller Solomon (Cambridge, Mass., 1969), 1: 185, 2: 323.

19. Timothy Pickering, *A Review of the Correspondence between . . . John Adams . . . and the Late William Cunningham* (Salem, 1824), 4, 90–91; Pickering, *Observations Introductory to the Reading of the Declaration of Independence at Salem July 4th, 1823* (Salem, 1823); Pickering to Marshall, December 26, 1828. Cullen, ed., *Papers of Marshall*, 2: 302. Pickering's dying thoughts on history are quoted in Clarfield, *Pickering*, 269. Despite his anger at Adams's remarks to Cunningham, Jefferson forgave Adams. Adams was delighted. Both men had been upset at

Pickering's show of animosity. See Malone, *Jefferson and His Time*, vol. 6: *Sage of Monticello* (Boston, 1981), 434–35.

20. Jefferson to John Holmes, April 22, 1820, Lipscomb and Bergh, eds., *Writings of Jefferson*, 15: 250; Madison, "Advice to My Country" (1836), Hunt, ed., *Writings*, 9: 610A-B. Madison's final struggle to deal with sectionalism, slavery, and agricultural self-sufficiency in the Old Dominion are traced in Ralph Ketcham, *James Madison: A Biography* (New York, 1971), 623–46.

21. One finds all the denial, anger, and depression of the old revolutionaries in the aged ill today; see Elisabeth Kübler-Ross, "Facing Death," in John G. Howells, ed., *Modern Perspectives in the Psychiatry of Old Age* (New York, 1975), 531–40. And today, as then, the study of one's own history can be therapeutic; Donald J. Dietrich, "Psychohistory," *Historical Method* 15 (1982): 88.

22. Brackenridge, Introduction to *Collected [Gazette] Essays* (1805), in Marder, ed., *Brackenridge Reader*, 353–54; Brackenridge, *Modern Chivalry*, 4 [1815]: 803. On Brackenridge's personal appearance, see Marder, *Brackenridge*, 60–61.

23. Jefferson, January 6, 1821, *Autobiography*, 19; Jefferson to Madison, February 27, 1826, Ford, ed., *Writings of Jefferson*, 10: 378; Jefferson to Roger C. Weightman, June 24, 1826, Lipscomb and Bergh, eds., *Writings of Jefferson*, 16: 181–82.

24. Adams to Jefferson, May 16, 1815, Adams Papers, Massachusetts Historical Society. Adams's emotions can be seen in his letter to Mercy Otis Warren, November 24, 1813, in "Warren-Adams Letters, II," *Massachusetts Historical Society Collections* 73 (Boston, 1925), 388. Adams was a prolific historical epistletor in his old age; see Howe, *The Changing Political Thought of John Adams*, 217–52, and Shaw, *Character of Adams*, 287–94.

25. Rufus King, "Speech to the Senate, March 18, 1824," in King, ed., *Life and Correspondence of Rufus King*, 6: 709–10. He knew that was his valedictory address; see Ernst, *King*, 389.

26. Madison to Drake, January 12, 1835, Hunt, ed., *Writings*, 9: 546; Madison to ———, March 1836, *Writings*, 9: 610; see also Ketcham, *Madison*, 660–64.

27. Marshall to Story, September 30, 1829, Oster, ed., *Political and Economic Doctrines of Marshall*, 129–30; Marshall to John Marshall, Jr., December 7, 1834, *Doctrines of Marshall*, 56. And see Leonard Baker, *John Marshall: A Life in Law* (New York, 1974), 766.

28. Philip Freneau, "A Midnight Storm in the Gulph Stream" (1822), "The Great Western Canal" (1822), "Winter" (1827), in Lewis Leary,

ed., *The Last Poems of Philip Freneau* (New Brunswick, 1945), 86, 21, 123. The note to his son-in-law Freneau jotted on the flyleaf of a collection of his poems (Axelrod, *Freneau*, 417).

29. Becker, *Denial of Death*, 260–85.

CONCLUSION

1. Erik Erikson, "Human Strength and the Cycle of Generations," in *Insight and Responsibility* (New York, 1964), 122–34.

2. Erikson, "Human Strength and the Cycle of Generations," 155–56; Erikson, *Dimensions of a New Identity*, 75–83.

Note on Method and Materials

Psychohistory has always been controversial, and no one takes more delight in critical analysis of psychohistorical methods than psychohistorians. Although the trench warfare between the Freudians and their critics—witness the response to David Stannard's *Shrinking History* (New York, 1981) and the reception of recent psychobiographies of Richard Nixon and Jimmy Carter—outguns any controversy *Revolution and Regeneration* might trigger, I have already been warned by one co-worker: "How can you use Erikson without mentioning the 'unconscious.'" While no historian can turn a deaf ear to those working in his own field, I have tried to approach problems to method in a commonsense fashion. I began with my subject, not with my method, and asked whether such figures as Hamilton and Madison really passed through recognizable stages of life. It seemed safe to say that a group of young men entering a great political contest while suspended between their parents' homes and the outside world had a good deal in common, but were these shared experiences of motivation—these experiments with personal freedom and adult responsibility—as compelling to them as they are to us? Indeed, was their sequence of maturation the same as ours? It is tempting to assume that, unless there is pathological regression to more infantile behavior (conduct rarely seen among the better-known revolutionaries, for obvious reasons), the historian may expect a progression from youthful pursuits to the self-accounting of old age. The major objection to this straightforward approach is the culture-boundedness of modern psychological concepts. Erikson concedes this danger (*Childhood and Society*, 122–23), but his concession does not deflect the accusation. One answer is to let the reader compare different psychohistorical approaches and decide which of them, if any, appears historical-minded, but even the most adept collection—a superb example is Robert J. Brugger, ed., *Our Selves, Our Past: Psychological Approaches to American History* (Baltimore, 1981)—cannot allay some readers' doubts that twentieth-century psychology can explain eighteenth-century motivation.

Life-cycle psychohistory avoids some of this criticism by resting upon *two* methodological foundations: developmental psychology of motivation (which we have discussed in the introduction to this book) and life-cycle history. By tying the first to historical research in the second, we can surmount the obstacle of culture-boundedness. The following pages present a very select bibliography of works in life-cycle history, works that have critically affected the argument in *Revolution and Regeneration*.

The historical study of life cycle begins with investigation of family history. Over the past decade, historical demographers and students of "life course" have explored the relationship between family composition and emotional maturation. Summaries of this literature can be found in Tamara K. Hareven, "The Last Stage: Historical Adulthood and Old Age," in Erik Erikson, ed., *Adulthood* (New York, 1978), 201–5; Tamara K. Hareven, ed., *Transitions* (New York, 1978); and Daniel Scott Smith, "The Estimates of Early American Historical Demographers: Two Steps Forward, One Step Back, What Steps in the Future?" *Historical Methods* 12 (Winter 1979): 24–38. Social historians, drawing upon cross-sectional studies of population and family, have fashioned longitudinal analyses of social attitudes toward the stages of life. On childhood and youth in early America, I recommend Nancy F. Cott, "Notes toward an Interpretation of Antebellum Childbearing," *Psychohistory Review* 6 (Spring 1978): 4–20; John Demos, *A Little Commonwealth: Family Life in Plymouth Colony* (New York, 1970); John Demos, *Entertaining Satan: Witchcraft and the Culture of Early New England* (New York, 1982); and Philip J. Greven, Jr., *The Protestant Temperament: Patterns of Childbearing, Religious Experience, and the Self in Early America* (New York, 1977). A rapidly growing literature on attitudes toward old age is crowned by W. Andrew Aschenbaum, *Old Age in the New Land* (Baltimore, 1978); David H. Fischer, *Growing Old in America* (New York, 1978); and Daniel Scott Smith, "Old Age and the 'Great Transformation': A New England Case Study," in Stuart F. Spicker et al., eds., *Aging and the Elderly: Humanistic Perspectives in Gerontology* (Atlanta Highlands, N.J., 1978), 285–302. A review of the literature is Matilda W. Riley, "Aging, Social Change, and the Power of Ideas," *Daedalus* (Fall 1978): 39–52. All of these interpretive essays give breadth to the demographers' data and the family historians' insights.

A handful of intrepid scholars have ventured to explain what changes in attitudes and status toward life cycle have meant to the young and the old: life cycle from the inside. This is a more exciting and speculative form of life-cycle history than the study of attitudes toward life stages, for the former rests on the historian's perception of human traits across a gulf of space and time. The pathbreaking work in this field was accomplished by Philippe Ariès and presented in his *Centuries of Childhood: A Social History of Family Life*, trans. Robert Baldick (New York, 1962), *Western Attitudes toward Death, from the Middle Ages to the Present*, trans. Patricia M. Ranum (Baltimore, 1974), and *The Hour of Our Death*, trans. Helen Weaver (New York, 1981). Coupling Ariès's and others' insights (including those of Erikson) to demographic and family history, American scholars have ventured into the subjective, internal realm of life cycle. Examples of their conclusions are found in Daniel Scott Smith, "Parental Power and Marriage Patterns: An Analysis of Historical Trends in Hingham, Massachusetts," *Journal of Marriage and the Family* 35 (1973): 419–28; Daniel Scott Smith and Michael Hindus, "Premarital Pregnancy in America, 1640–1971: An Overview and Interpretation" *Journal of Interdisciplinary History* 5 (Spring 1975): 536–80; John Demos and Virginia Demos, "Adolescence in Historical Perspective," *Journal of Marriage and the Family* 31 (November 1969): 632–54; N. Ray Hiner, "Adolescence in Eighteenth Century America," *History of Childhood Quarterly* 2 (1975): 253–80; and Joseph F. Kett, *Rites of Passage: Adolescence in America 1790 to the Present* (New York, 1979).

The prospects for success of life-cycle psychohistory thus depend on the historian's willingness and ability to adjust the psychological model to the place and time of his study. In the present case, even if general movement from one stage to the next in eighteenth- and early nineteenth-century America parallels that in modern America, we must concede that the emotional content and social customs surrounding the stages varied from that age to our own. The greatest variations lay in adolescence and old age. Our own century is the era of youth, in which we have come to lionize the tastes and habits of the young. There is some question whether our eighteenth-century predecessors even recognized the concept of adolescence, although by the late 1600s parents, ministers, and teachers recognized some special problems in later childhood. Childhood completed, the young man was expected to marry, enter a career, conduct his affairs and rear his children responsibly, and later to pass on his wisdom to another generation. At the other end of the scale, old age carried far more respectability and influence in the eighteenth century than it does today. The patriarch held sway in the family, the church, and the town meeting. The old had proved their power over nature by cheating death. They were repositories of oral lore, experience, and moral virtue. Their control of their children under the law and in practical matters of marriage, property settlements, and career was formidable. The nineteenth century would see erosion of these powers and the status that accompanied them, a process begun before the last of the Founding Fathers died, causing them to lament more keenly their failing powers. This shift in objective status would exacerbate the agonies of stocktaking but not change the need to reassess one's life. Judging from the bitter self-recrimination of their final historical remarks, one can say the old revolutionaries knew they had lost much of their influence and status.

Rooted in sensible use of life-cycle research, nurtured by the periodic appearance of full-scale life-cycle biographies—most recently Carol M. Petillo, *Douglas MacArthur: The Philippine Years* (Bloomington, Ind., 1981)—the field of life-cycle psychohistory is growing steadily. By the time this brief notice of indebtedness appears in print some of its readers will have moved beyond my own contribution. Nevertheless, even a limited and dated essay on sources foretells a long and successful marriage of life-cycle research and psychohistorical writing.

Index

Index

Education, and ideas of revolutionary generation of 1776, 70–73
Elkins, Stanley, 5
Erickson, Erick, 2, 3, 8, 116, 117, 133–34, 142 (n. 32), 157, 158. See also Life cycle

Fame, as theme in history, 37–38, 102. See also Revolutionary generation, and use of history
Family, and study of history, 158–59. See also Psychohistory, and family
Father figure, 26, 34, 97; and king, 33, 34; as founders of the republic, 72, 73, 75. See also Revolutionary generation
Federalism. See Constitution, federal; Party, federalist (pro-Constitution)
Fenno, John, 88
Filiopietism, as theme in writing, 119–22
Fischer, David Hackett, 4, 119
France, 73, 74, 90. See also Revolution, in France
Franklin, Benjamin, 20, 102
Freneau, Philip, 6, 16, 33, 46, 49, 79, 80, 128–29

Galloway, Joseph, 22
Generation: as tool of historical analysis, 4–6, 8–9, 135 (n. 4); older than revolutionaries of 1776, 18–23, 63; younger than revolutionaries of 1776, 83, 85, 105, 110. See also Revolutionary generation
Genius, of Americans, 36–37, 132
Gerry, Elbridge, 6, 30, 48, 98; Observations on the Constitution, 60
Giles, William Branch, 85
Gorham, John, 61
Greece, 56, 59, 61, 64

Hamilton, Alexander, 6, 16, 27, 30, 48, 56, 67, 68, 81, 88, 96, 97–98, 102, 103, 114; Federalist Papers, 59–60; Letter Concerning . . . John Adams, 106–7. See also Party, Federalist
Henry, Patrick, 21, 63–65
History: as discipline, 10, 30, 43, 72–73, 103–4, 115–16, 130, 131–32; of America, 11, 35, 58, 75, 111, 118; Whig laws of, 11, 14, 18, 32, 40–69 passim, 82; American separate from English, 14–39 passim; provincial, 18–22; of England, 21; American incomparable to any other, 50–69 passim; partisan, 75–101 passim, 102, 104, 106, 114–15; as process, 76, 78, 82, 84, 88; as order, 76, 92–96, 97; renunciation of, 104–30 passim; patriotic, 110. See also Puritanism, and ideas of history
Humphreys, David, 6, 36, 45, 87, 95, 119, 120, 121; Anarchiad, 45
Hutchinson, Thomas, 19, 20, 82

Independence, 14, 23, 36, 39, 44. See also Declaration of Independence

Jackson, Andrew, 5
Jay, John, 6, 22, 37, 42, 50, 58, 67, 89, 111
Jay Treaty, 80, 81
Jefferson, Thomas, 6, 23, 28, 29, 33, 35, 42, 46, 48, 66, 67, 70, 73, 76, 78, 79, 80, 81, 87, 96, 103, 106, 112, 113, 116, 117, 118, 122–23, 125–26, 148 (n. 9), 154 (n. 19); A Summary View of the Rights of British America, 17, 35; Notes on the State of Virginia, 53–54; Kentucky Resolutions, 84; "Anas," 113, 114

Kammen, Michael, 14, 76

Index

Index